THE ELEMENTS OF CONDUCTING

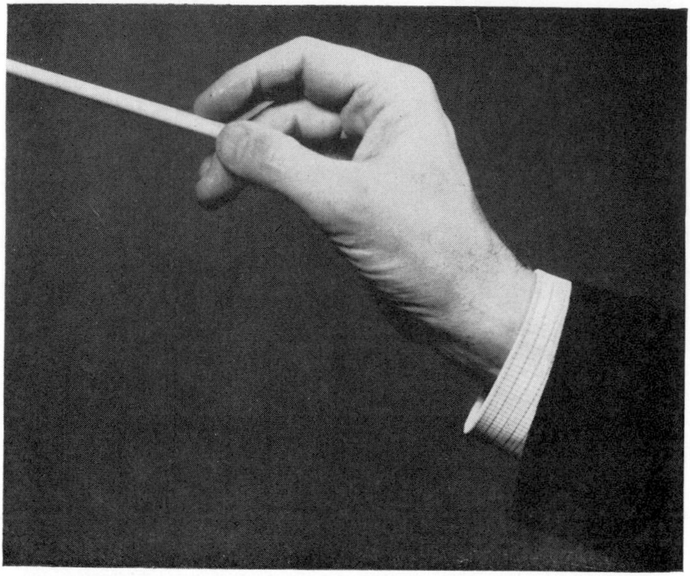

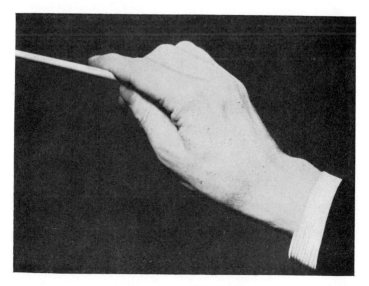

FIGURE 6—CORRECT

FIGURE 7—CRAMPED

THE BATON

WILLIAM COX-IFE

THE
ELEMENTS OF
CONDUCTING

FOREWORD BY
SIR ADRIAN BOULT

THE JOHN DAY COMPANY
NEW YORK

FOREWORD

BY SIR ADRIAN BOULT

ELSEWHERE recently I had occasion to comment on the fact that the art of conducting was altogether so new that it had not yet had time to canalise into the various schools and methods which we hear so much about in connection with the art and technique of singing and the playing of instruments.

Within a few weeks of the publication of those remarks Mr Cox-Ife has shown me another perfect example to prove my point. I am sure that he would agree that his many solutions to problems are not necessarily the only ones possible, and, as he goes into a great deal of detail, particularly in regard to the movements of the point of the stick, he would admit alternatives; indeed he himself gives examples of two different ways of conducting six in a bar, and I emphatically agree with his expression of preference in this matter.

The later chapters of the book include much wisdom on such subjects as accompanying, style, homework, rehearsals, and in particular a wealth of useful information about everything to do with light opera. Here, to the best of my knowledge, Mr Cox-Ife is exploring ground that has never been covered before, and, as this field is immensely popular all over this country, many conductors will be specially grateful for a detailed examination of their problems by one who has had great experience and can put his points clearly and succinctly.

CONTENTS

AUTHOR'S PREFACE

IN spite of the surfeit of 'ready-made' music of every kind
that is available today, groups of 'do-it-yourself' enthusiasts are to be found in every community. These groups
vary in size and technical ability, but they all have in
common the urge to 'make' music rather than be satisfied
to sit back in a comfortable chair and let the record-player
or radio do all the work.

I have, in my travels both at home and in the U.S.A.,
heard a great number of these groups at work; sometimes
it has been a full-sized symphony orchestra, at other times
a small bunch of enthusiasts joyfully ploughing their way
through a Gilbert and Sullivan opera. Between these two
extremes I have heard societies of every type and size perform, with abounding energy, and a considerable sense of
achievement and great enjoyment, a wide variety of music.

As a professional musician of many years' experience I
am all for this 'do-it-yourself' music-making, which must
be encouraged by all, as it is a truly vital contribution to
the life of any community. I do recall, however, being
present on occasions when the aspirations of all concerned
were sadly hampered by the faulty baton technique of the
conductor.

No matter how keen and efficient are the players or
singers, they do need firm and unequivocal direction when
performing. The clearer the beat the more confident they
will be and so will the result be more in accordance with
their intentions. I know, from personal experience, how
difficult it is to perform a work, no matter how well one
knows it, under an ambiguous or hesitant baton.

There are a few excellent and exhaustive studies on the

technique of orchestral conducting, but these have obviously been written for the student who hopes to become a professional conductor rather than for the enthusiastic amateur.

Of course, it has been said that conductors are born, not made, and it is true that in the past there were great conductors who had evolved their technique through the tiresome method of 'trial and error'. I remember being told, when a student, some incredible stories of the early performance of the $\frac{5}{4}$ movement from the 'Pathetique' Symphony, when inexperienced conductors were faced for the first time with this revolutionary time signature.

It is now an accepted fact that there is a technique of handling a baton that can be acquired by careful study, as can be the technique of any musical instrument. It is no longer good enough to be a fine musician and have a flair for 'wielding the stick'! This was made abundantly clear by my teacher, the late Sir Henry J. Wood, who insisted that certain fundamental rules should always be borne in mind and adhered to by he who was 'on the box'.

More than one orchestral player of note has told me that it was possible to step in at the last minute and play an unfamiliar work with absolute confidence under Sir Henry, because his baton technique was so clear that, providing one kept an eye on the beat, it was difficult to go wrong.

Now if it is important to a thoroughly experienced musician to get a good, clear beat from the conductor, how much more important is this to the amateur instrumentalist?

In the chapters which follow will be found basic rules of giving a clear, firm and expressive beat which is the foundation of conducting. It is, of course, clearly to be understood that 'wagging the stick' is only part of the conductor's art, albeit a very important part. There is also, not only general musicianship, but a knowledge of the orchestral instruments and singing, both solo and choral, which a good conductor must possess. Not forgetting the ability to inspire and lead, without which all of the afore-mentioned attributes are as nothing.

But rather than discuss these matters which have been written about many times, I have chosen to include some chapters on the problems of conducting light opera and 'musicals'. I KNOW OF NO BOOK WHICH OFFERS ANY ADVICE FOR THE CONDUCTOR OF THIS TYPE OF MUSIC.

Conducting in the theatre, whether it is grand opera or 'musical', is very different from conducting in the concert hall, and presents many additional problems which it is the responsibility of the conductor to resolve.

Where reference in the text has been made to the standard scores of the classical, operatic, and orchestral repertory, this reference is to the scores themselves as stated, and the reader desiring to make acquaintance with them can consult the many excellent scores now available of these works.

1

The Baton

TYPES AND SUGGESTIONS
AS TO CHOICE

THERE are many types of baton on sale in any good music shop and the choice is one of personal preference. I myself, prefer a short baton although, when a student, my teacher, Sir Henry J. Wood, preferred me to use a long one. Should a long baton be used, the important thing is that it must be light and rigid, so that the tip does not waggle or 'whip'. This cannot happen if a short baton is used. The shape of the handle also depends upon the user's preference.

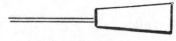

FIGURE I

This large cork handle is very comfortable, but is only found, as a rule, on a long baton.

FIGURE 2

This ball-shaped handle, also of cork, is very comfortable, but can take a little getting used to.

FIGURE 3

This type of baton is made all in one piece and is used by many well-known conductors. I was warned by Sir Henry that if held in a strong grip it could lead to aching hand muscles. But I have used this type of baton many times and found it most comfortable.

I suggest for work in the ordinary theatre pit, with its limitations of space, a baton that is no longer than 14 inches.

FIGURE 4

The baton should not weigh more than one ounce. In the case of a ball handle the point of balance should be about one inch from the upper end of the handle, Fig. 5a. The point of balance in the case of the baton with a large handle falls at the top end of the handle itself, Fig. 5b.

POINT OF BALANCE   POINT OF BALANCE

FIGURE 5a   FIGURE 5b

A short baton, too, is less liable to be broken.

HOW TO HOLD THE BATON

Before this can be discussed, one must appreciate the exact function of the baton. Perhaps the best definition of this is given by Malko when he says that the baton is, in effect, an 'extension of one's first finger'.

The baton is primarily used to indicate the exact moment at which each beat of the bar falls due. This being so, it is obvious that it is the tip of the baton which marks these divisions in time. This is something that must never be forgotten by any conductor. How many times was Sir Henry heard to say: 'Every eye, please — every eye on the tip of the baton.' This to orchestral players as well as singers!

No matter what type of baton is used the correct way of holding it is the same; lightly at the point of balance by the thumb, first and second fingers, as shown in Fig. 6 (frontispiece). This method will permit a free movement of the wrist, which is necessary to give a precise beat.

The kind of hold shown in Fig. 7 (frontispiece) definitely cramps the style of any but a great conductor, but they, naturally, are a law unto themselves.

HOW TO GIVE A CLEAR BEAT

Having become accustomed to the 'feel' of the baton, the next task is to learn to give a clear beat. This can be done in three different ways.

First by a movement of the wrist.

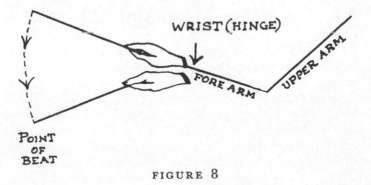

FIGURE 8

Secondly by a movement of the forearm.

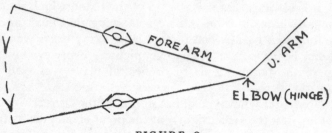

FIGURE 9

Thirdly by using the whole arm.

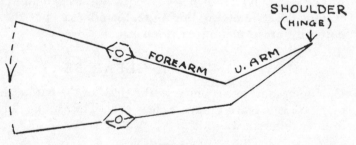

FIGURE 10

N.B. In the second and third methods there should also be a slight 'give' at the wrist, but no suggestion of flabbiness. In the third method the elbow, too, 'gives' very slightly. Neither wrist nor elbow should ever be held rigid at any time.

Practise these three movements until they can be made without any stiffness or rigidity in either muscles or joints and the baton moved up and down with a free, easy, but controlled movement. Do not forget the warning about the tip of the baton indicating the point of each beat.

I suggest that these elementary exercises are first practised sitting down, for then the mind can concentrate on the arm only.

Finally these exercises will have to be done standing up. The stance when conducting is of great importance, for a conductor must be able not only to stand for long periods, but to turn his body easily from the waist, from left to right, in order, on special occasions, to control the players on either side of the concert platform or stage, or in the theatre pit. It is rarely that a conductor should turn his whole body; the movement is usually confined to the torso.

Learn to stand with the weight of the body evenly distributed on both feet, which should be about twelve inches apart. The whole body should be relaxed and any movement confined to the arms.

One word of warning. Avoid from the outset any tendency to 'stomp about' when conducting. In the concert hall you will be liable to fall off the podium and in the theatre pit there will be no room. I remember overhearing at a rehearsal an orchestral player, who had given a quick glance at where the conductor (one of the stomping kind) should have been, murmur: 'Now where the hell has he got to? As if it mattered?' Do not let that be said about you.

2

Basic Time-beating—1

A L L time-beating is based upon certain fundamental patterns described by the baton, which indicate one, two, three or four beats in the bar. In the case of compound time, e.g. $\frac{9}{8}$ or $\frac{12}{8}$, the basic pattern of the three and four beats remains unchanged, although each beat may be subdivided. When more complicated time signatures are met with, such as $\frac{5}{4}$, $\frac{7}{4}$, $\frac{10}{4}$ or $\frac{11}{4}$ etc., the patterns described by the baton will be a combination of two or more of the basic shapes. $\frac{5}{4}$ is $\frac{3}{4} + \frac{2}{4}$ or vice versa. A seven beat can be built upon a broad three-beat pattern subdivided into 2 + 2 + 3 or on a four-pattern of 2 + 2 + 2 + 1.

I have only touched briefly upon these more complicated rhythms, as it is very rarely that the amateur conductor will find himself involved with such music. But there is one example over which many amateur conductors have stumbled and that is Jack Point's entrance in the *Yeomen of the Guard*, by Sullivan. Here, I believe for the first time in operetta of the period, the time signature of $\frac{5}{4}$ was used in rhythmic phrases which also included bars in $\frac{4}{4}$ and $\frac{3}{4}$ time. This will be discussed fully in due course.

To beat one in a bar the baton moves from A to B and back again. The point or 'click' of the beat which marks the precise moment at which the beat falls due is at B. The baton returning, as a reflex action, to A, from whence it moves immediately back to B for the next bar.

1   *One in a bar*

¢ *presto,* $\frac{2}{4}, \frac{3}{8}, \frac{3}{4}.$

FIGURE 11

N.B. From the diagram it would appear that the return of the baton is on a path a little to the left of the downward passage. This is not so, for in practice the baton should return on exactly the same path as it descended. Obviously this cannot be shown in a diagram, hence the apparent discrepancy.

At the point of the beat (B), when a fast tempo is being indicated, the movement of the baton is as if it had struck a piece of stretched elastic which causes it to rebound to A.

It is at this early stage that I would impress upon all would-be conductors a golden rule that should rarely be ignored. It is this: *On the first beat of the bar the baton should come straight down.*

Speaking from personal experience I know how disconcerting it is to work under anyone who disregards (if ever they knew) this rule.

2   *Two in a bar*

¢, $\frac{2}{4}$, $\frac{6}{8}$.

FIGURE 12

For the first beat the baton travels from A to B. The reflex action at the point of the beat at B is a small one and the baton moves to C for the second beat and then straight back to A for the first beat of the next bar. The movement from A to B is fast and from B to C comparatively slow, as there is a much smaller distance for the baton to travel. Do not, at this stage, allow the baton to stop between B and C, for this would indicate either a pause* or a *staccato* articulation of the music; matters which will be dealt with later. This holds good for all time beating.

A word of warning here. Do not allow the reflex action or rebound at B to be too high. Should this happen the baton will travel thus

*Fermata.

FIGURE 13

and there will be a danger of the movement towards the second beat at C being mistaken for a down beat, i.e. the first beat of a bar. This control of the rebound should be observed at all times.

3   *Three in a bar*

$\frac{3}{2}, \frac{3}{4}, \frac{9}{8}.$

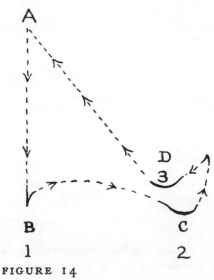

FIGURE 14

Whenever conducting three in a bar, at whatever speed, the field of beating should be based upon this shape.

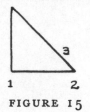

FIGURE 15

It should be observed, however, that the speed between C and D is slower than between A and B, and B and C.

4   *Four in a bar*

C, $\frac{4}{4}$, $\frac{12}{8}$.

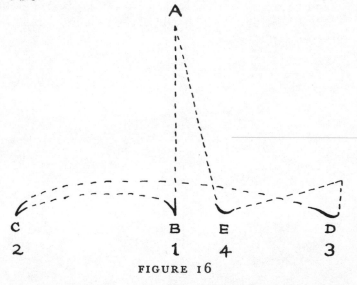

FIGURE 16

In beating four in a bar the point of the fourth beat can be shown nearer to that of the third beat, but placed where

I have put it will result in a very clear 'up beat' to the first beat of the next bar. So I suggest that this is the basic shape to keep in mind when beating quadruple time.

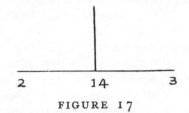

FIGURE 17

Be careful not to skimp the movement of the baton between the first and second beat (Fig. 16 B to C). If it is not directed well to the left of the body, it becomes difficult for the players to see exactly where the second beat falls and the basic shape of the field of beating will resemble that of three in a bar.

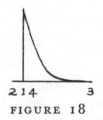

FIGURE 18

This was another of Sir Henry's insistent demands!

It may come as a surprise to the student that when making all of these movements with the wrist only the baton will travel a distance of nearly 16 inches from A to B and B to C and about 30 inches from C to D. This is quite a considerable field to cover, so it can be seen how careful one must be, when using the arms, not to give too big a beat. Orchestras don't take kindly to windmill conductors and, unlike Don Quixote, the players can 'tilt' with good effect!

Practise the foregoing movements using wrist, forearm and whole arm, until clear patterns can be described with a flowing *legato* movement between each beat. Then repeat, using the forearm and marking the point of each beat by a very slight movement of the wrist. Next practise all the movements using wrist, forearm and whole arm, stopping the baton at each point of beat before moving on to the next beat. Do this exercise first with a light *staccato* beat and then with a more forceful *marcato* beat.

Start practising slowly, say ♩ = 72 and gradually increase the speed to ♩ = 92. When this range of speed is mastered try slower as well as faster tempi.

Here is a word of advice on how to acquire a *steady* beat, for nothing is more disconcerting to both performers and audience than a conductor who runs away with the music. Practising with that bugbear of our early days, the metronome, can be very boring, so why not get some records of marches played by regimental bands and waltzes played by one of the 'strict tempo' dance bands, and practise to these? Remember, however, that records should not be used until a certain facility in beating time has been acquired.

Finally, in describing the foregoing patterns the baton must be clearly visible to the performers and the patterns themselves of such clear definition that they are easily understood by all concerned.

3

Basic Time-beating—2

THE next stage to master is that of subdividing the beat. This is necessary when conducting very slow movements or one in which it is difficult to obtain absolute precision with the single beat and also for controlling a marked *rallentando* or *ritenuto*.

It is quite simple to do. Just repeat, with a small gesture, the movement of the tip of the baton at the point of the beat, once or twice as the case demands.

1 *Subdividing in simple time*

₵ or ⅔.

FIGURE 19

N.B. Although the diagram is drawn thus, all the movements of the baton are made on the same path as that of the down beat.

Subdivision is a repetition 'on the spot' and not an additional pattern made to one side or the other of the original point of beat.

MUSIC EXAMPLES

Haydn: 'London' Symphony, *Andante*.
Haydn: 'Surprise' Symphony, *Andante*.
Elgar: Serenade for Strings, *Larghetto*.

2    $\frac{3}{2}$ *or* $\frac{3}{4}$

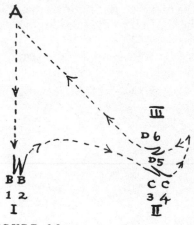

FIGURE 20

MUSIC EXAMPLES

Bach: Brandenburg Concerto No. 6, *Adagio*.
Bach: Klavier Concerto D Min., *Adagio*.
Beethoven: *Egmont* Overture.
Bizet: 'L'Arlésienne' Suite No. 1, *Adagietto*.
Mozart: Symphony in C (K 425), *Adagio*.

3 $\frac{4}{4}$

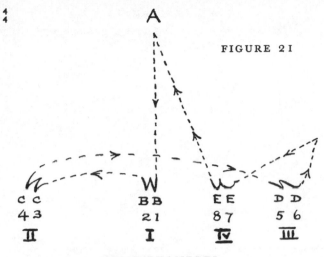

FIGURE 21

MUSIC EXAMPLES

Rossini: *Barber of Seville* Overture.
Beethoven: Symphony No. 1, *Adagio molto* (bars 1–12).
Weber: *Oberon* Overture, *Adagio sostenuto*.
German: *Merrie England, Largamente* (vs*, p. 149).

4   *Subdividing in compound time*

$\frac{9}{8}$

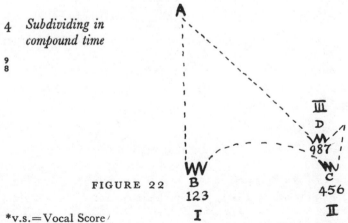

FIGURE 22

*v.s. = Vocal Score

MUSIC EXAMPLE

Debussy: *Prélude à l'après-midi d'un faune*, MIN. SC.,
P. 30, bar 1.

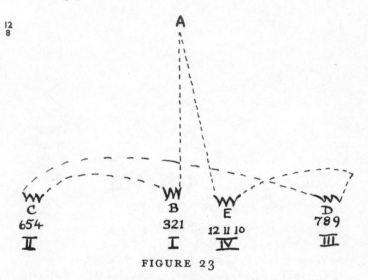

FIGURE 23

MUSIC EXAMPLE

Bach: Concerto for two violins, *Largo non tanto*.

*Remember that when subdividing the beat throughout the whole
bar the basic shape of the field of beat (see Figs. 15 and 17) should
still be clearly defined.* It is also advisable when subdividing in
either two or three, to mark the secondary beats a little less
strongly than the primary ones.

5   *Subdividing in ⁶₈ time*

Although ⁶₈ is compound duple time, the subdivision of the
beats upon the lines suggested for triple and quadruple
time will not be satisfactory. It is better to regard ⁶₈, when
not beaten two in a bar, as a special case and to be studied
as such.

There are two accepted ways of beating six in a bar — the German and Italian. I have always found that a modified version of the German method is one which serves the majority of cases where six in a bar is called for.

This is the pattern that I use:

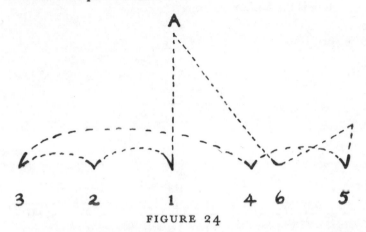

FIGURE 24

The great advantage in using this pattern is the clear division of the half bar which prevents any wavering rhythm. The anchor points of six in a bar, one and four, are very easily seen.

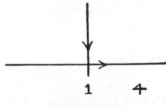

FIGURE 25

I strongly advise the student to use this pattern as a general rule. If later he cares to learn the Italian pattern he may, but I do not feel that it is as good as the German.

It is said, on excellent authority, that the Italian pattern is better for the tempi which have to be beaten in a quick six rather than a steady or slow, two. Even in such cases I still have found that the German method, using small gestures, is perfectly satisfactory.

Here is the Italian pattern:

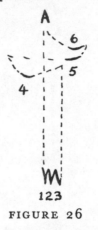

FIGURE 26

This pattern, unless extremely neatly executed, can get muddly on the fourth, fifth and sixth beats; something that never happens when the German pattern is used.

EXERCISES

2. ADAGIO ♩ = 66 . SUBDIVIDE THE BEAT THROUGHOUT.

(musical notation)

3. ALLEGRO MODERATO ♩ = 100

(musical notation)

Earlier I said that $\frac{5}{4}$ time was beaten as $2 + 3$ or $3 + 2$ in the bar, and referred to Sullivan's opera which has music of this rhythmic pattern. Exercise 3 is adapted from this music of Sullivan's, but instead of writing a bar in $\frac{5}{4}$ I have written two bars, one in $\frac{2}{4}$ and the other in $\frac{3}{4}$. To beat a bar in $\frac{5}{4}$ time use this combination of the basic shapes of $\frac{2}{4}$ and $\frac{3}{4}$.

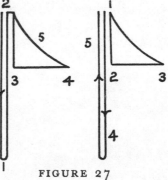

FIGURE 27

To conduct this number up to speed, *Allegro con brio*, beat upon the following lines.

vs, P. 49, second bar onwards:

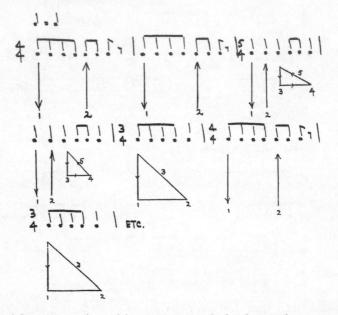

After mastering this sequence of rhythms, the young conductor should find no difficulty in directing the 'Bazaar of the Caravans', from *Kismet*, with the alternating bars in $\frac{3}{4}$ and $\frac{2}{4}$.

4

Starting and Stopping

ALTHOUGH the student has assuredly mastered by now the exercises given in the previous chapters, he will still be unable to stand in front of a group of players and take them through even a simple piece of music satisfactorily, for he has yet to learn how to 'start them off'.

This can be the cause of some heart-burning not only to novice conductors but to experienced orchestral players who, quite rightly, expect as well as need a good clear beat so that they can start with confidence and accord. A good start depends solely upon the conductor's ability to give a clear preparatory beat.

Here is a perfectly simple rule which, if obeyed, will solve this problem to everyone's satisfaction. It was drummed into us by Sir Henry until a good up beat (as it is commonly known) became a conditioned reflex.

The conductor must give, in strict tempo, the complete beat which immediately precedes the beat upon which the music commences.

The easiest preparatory beat to give is the one which precedes music which commences on the first beat of the bar. Whatever the time signature of the music concerned, this preparatory beat is always the same.

A to B is the path of the baton for the first beat of the bar. x to A marks the path of the preparatory beat.

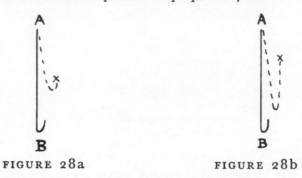

FIGURE 28a   FIGURE 28b

Do not sweep right down as in Fig. 28b, for such a movement of the baton might be confused with, or mistaken for, the down beat proper and trap someone into making a false entry. Even in music which is one in a bar the preparatory beat is still the same, except that it is better to start it lower down, on a level with B, but be sure to give it a strong upward sweep.

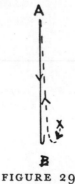

FIGURE 29

N.B. Although the 'up beat' has always to be precise, it is negative in character and carries no visual command to play.

Starting on the second beat of the bar

The preparatory beat for music which starts on the second beat of the bar, no matter what the time signature is, is always a down beat.

There are, however, two modifications to be made. Firstly the baton starts this preparatory beat with a small upward curve thus:

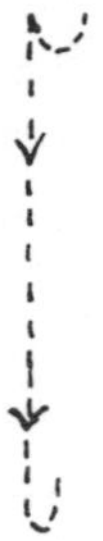

FIGURE 30

This tiny movement has the effect of getting the baton going and is really a minute 'up beat' to the preparatory beat. Secondly, this preparatory 'down beat' should not be as large as the subsequent positive beats.

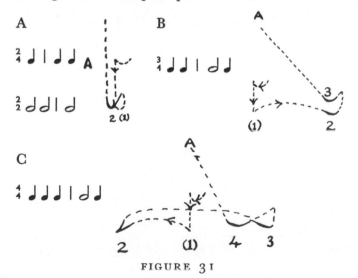

FIGURE 31

MUSIC EXAMPLES

A   Bach: Suite in B min., 'Badinerie'.
    Haydn: 'Surprise' Symphony, *Allegro di molto.*
    Mozart: 'Serenade in B♭', *Rondo.*
    German: Raleigh's song (No. 5), *Merrie England.*
    Kern: En'tracte (No. 18), *Show Boat.*

B   Gluck: Chaconne, *Orpheus.*

C   Gluck: *Iphigenia in Aulis,* Overture.

Starting on the third beat of the bar

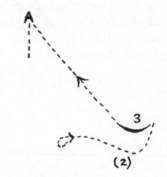

FIGURE 32

MUSIC EXAMPLES

Bach: Suite in B min., 'Sarabande'.
Mozart: 'Eine Kleine Nachtmusik', Minuet.
German: Quartet 'In England' (No. 16), *Merrie England.*
Berlin: Finale Act I (No. 23), *Annie Get Your Gun.*

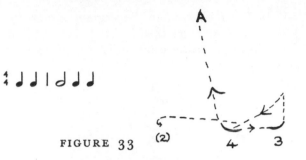

FIGURE 33

MUSIC EXAMPLES

Mozart: 'Eine Kleine Nachtmusik', Romance.
Sullivan: Gavotte, *The Gondoliers*.

Starting on the fourth beat of the bar

FIGURE 34

As the diagram shows, the preparatory beat starts centre R and the fourth beat is made more to the right than is shown in Fig. 16.

MUSIC EXAMPLES

Beethoven: Violin Concerto, *Larghetto*.
Bizet: Toreador's song, *Carmen*.
Sullivan: Overture, *The Pirates of Penzance*.
Rodgers: Duet Billy and Julie (No. 5), *Carousel*.

It will be found that when the student is more experienced in a case such as this $\frac{4}{4}$ ♩ | ♩ ♩ ♩. ♪ | *Allegro Moderato*, it appears to be quite sufficient to give a preparatory beat thus:

FIGURE 35

But, and this is a big 'but', such a beat, whilst offering a clear invitation to enter on the fourth beat of the bar, usually fails to indicate the speed of the movement. Therefore I suggest that this method is not acceptable as a general rule. Naturally there are exceptions where such a method is correct and these will be discussed in due course.

The preparatory beat and six in a bar

In music which is taken six in a bar it is quite simple to give a clear preparatory beat, no matter which beat the music starts on, providing the pattern of six in a bar (Fig. 24) is kept in mind.

MUSIC EXAMPLES

Sullivan: Overture, *Ruddigore*.
Mozart: Symphony in C (K 425), *Poco Adagio*.

Starting after the beat

In such cases ignore the notes which fall on the fraction of the beat and apply the rule given earlier in this chapter (p. 33).

EXERCISES

1. 𝄵 (♪) | ♩ ♩   2. ²/₄ (³♬♬) | ♩ ♫

3. ²/₄ (♬) | ♬♬♬ ♫ | 4. ³/₄ (♪) | ♩ ♩ |

5. ⁴/₄ (♪) | ♩ ♩ ♩ |
Prep. beat as Fig. 28a.

6. ²/₄ (♪) ♩ | ♩ ♩   7. ³/₄ (♪) ♩ | ♩ ♩ ♩ |

8. ⁴/₄ (♪) ♩ ♩ ♩ | ♩ ♫ ♩ |
Prep. beat as Fig. 31 A, B, C.

9. ³/₄ (♩♫) | ♩. ♫♫ | 10. ⁴/₄ (♪) ♫♫ ♩ | ♩ ♩ ♩ |
Prep. beat as Fig. 32.   Prep. beat as Fig. 33

11. ⁴/₄ (♪♪)♫ | ♩ ♩ ♩ | 12. ⁴/₄ (♪♪)♩ | ♩. ♪ ♩ |
Prep. beat as Fig. 34.   Prep. beat as Fig. 34.

It is inevitable that there will occur cases where this method doesn't work too well, especially with amateur players. A typical example is the commencement of the Rondo of Mozart's 'Eine Kleine Nachtmusik'.

ALLEGRO 𝄴 ♪ ♫♫ | ♩ ♩ ♩ ♩ | (2 in a bar).

According to the rule it is only necessary to give a clear up beat on two, to start the ball rolling, and with a fine body of players who know the work as well as, if not better, than the conductor this will probably work. But the entry of the first quaver* arrives so quickly after the baton begins to move that the ensemble can be very ragged. If this is the

*Eighth note.

case, don't keep on rehearsing; just give an extra preparatory beat thus:

and all will be well. This extra beat should be quite small, just done with the wrist and at the same time, the left hand holds an unobtrusive gesture of 'careful now'.

N.B. Whenever an extra beat is being given make sure that it is marked in the orchestral parts and the full score. Just '1 2' over the opening bar is all that is needed, and for heaven's sake do not get carried away at the performance and forget to give it. If you do, my young friend, the results will be disastrous.

As a guide as to when the extra beat is advisable, consider the speed (the quicker the music, the more difficult the entry) and how great a fraction of the opening beat is filled with notes. If, as in the Mozart, the beat is practically filled, then be prepared to offer this additional help. The dynamic Koussevitsky would always help a difficult entry this way.

Two other typical examples of the necessity for an extra beat are to be found in *Les Cloches de Corneville*, Planquette, 'Rondeau' (No. 2), and in *Merrie England*, Wilkin's song (No. 13).

Music starting with rests

When a piece of music starts with rests, or as we say 'the bar is written out', these rests must be beaten. If not, players who enter very much later will have been misled in their counting of the bars and be a bar behind when their entry falls due.

Sullivan: *Iolanthe*, VS, P. 153.

MAESTOSO ¾ ♪♪♩ | ♩. ♫♫ |

The gestures for the two crotchet* rests must be negative in character and quite small. Then with a strong third beat the orchestra will enter with complete confidence. Once more, use the left hand to hold a warning gesture on the silent beats. A raised finger is sufficient.

The non-metrical preparatory beat

When starting a very slow piece of music it is neither practical nor desirable to give one complete beat in strict time before the music commences. Either a half beat can be given, which corresponds to one of the subdivisions of the beat with which you will direct the movement, or a non-metrical beat (see Fig. 35) will be in order, as the players will be able to judge the tempo as the baton moves on the beat.

Weber: Overture, *Der Freischütz*.
Mozart: Overture, *Magic Flute*.
Sullivan: Overture, *H.M.S. Pinafore*.
Kismet Overture.

If the music starts on a pause the non-metrical beat is the only solution.

Beethoven: Overture, *Egmont*.
Mendelssohn: Overture, *Midsummer Night's Dream*.
Borodin: Symphony No. 2.

*Quarter note.

The final beat

And now, having been shown how to start, comes the problem of stopping. I shall only discuss here the final stop at the end of the music and not the momentary stop during the music.

First the *tutti* chord complete with pause.

MUSIC EXAMPLES

Weber: Overture, *Oberon*.
Mozart: Overture, *Don Giovanni*.

Such endings offer fine opportunities for a really dramatic gesture on the part of the conductor. But we mustn't forget that it is the players who are doing the work! Naturally the tension must not be allowed to sag and there must be a clean finish to the chord; just as important as was the clean start at the beginning. So hold the baton well up and still for the duration of the pause (Fig. 36)a and then give a steady preparatory gesture upwards before the baton is brought smartly down for the finish of the chord (Fig. 36)b.

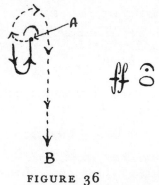

FIGURE 36

Next there are the finishes on a short chord.

MUSIC EXAMPLES

Mozart: Overture, *The Marriage of Figaro*.
Planquette: Overture, *Les Cloches de Corneville*.
Offenbach: Overture, *Orphée aux Enfers*.
Rodgers: Prologue, *Carousel*.
Sullivan: Lord Chancellor's song (VS, P. 180),
    Iolanthe.

In these cases just a clean swift downward stroke with the baton will suffice.

Now the *piano* endings. First on a pause marked *diminuendo*.

MUSIC EXAMPLES

Dvorak: New World Symphony.
Grieg: 'Death of Åse', *Peer Gynt*.
Sullivan: Quartet, 'Strange Adventure', *Yeomen of the Guard*.
Rodgers: 'What's the Use' (VS, P. 153), *Carousel*.

One down beat is given fairly high in the field of beating. Then the baton is brought slowly down, while the left hand is indicating *diminuendo*, and at the end a small, quiet finishing gesture is made.

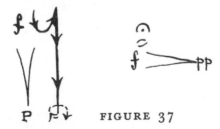

FIGURE 37

The finish on a short chord, *piano*, is indicated by a quiet, small gesture at the end of which the hand, or hands, are held quite still before they are gently lowered to the sides of the body.

5

Ebb and Flow—1

---

1   *The pause*

TO indicate a pause the baton is held quite still at the
point of the relevant beat. A small preparatory gesture is
given as the baton moves on again.

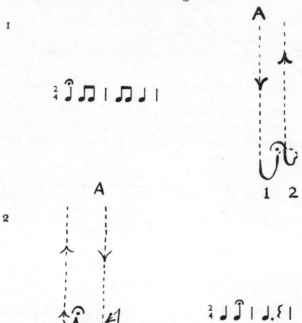

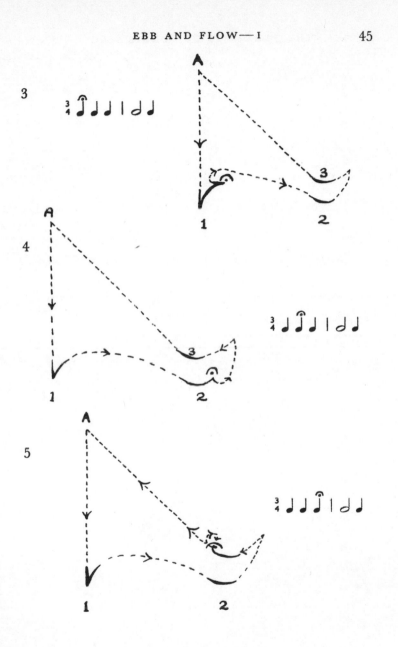

6

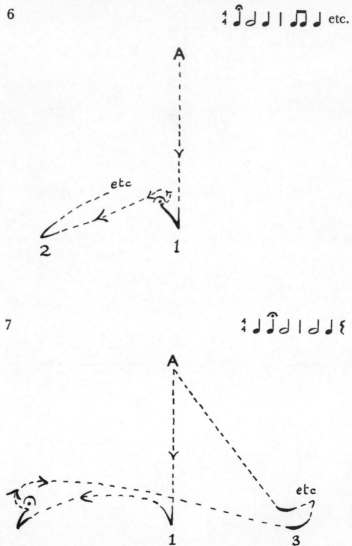

7

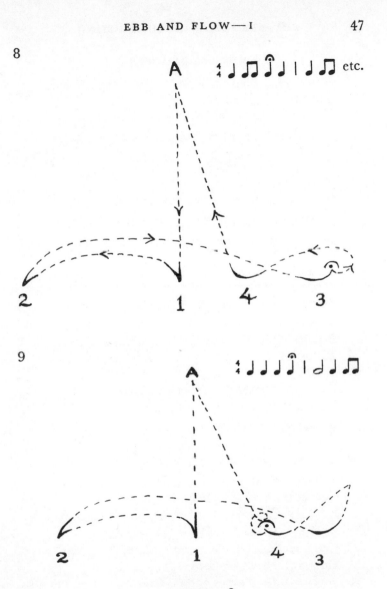

FIGURE 38

MUSIC EXAMPLES

1. Beethoven: Piano Concerto No. 1. Seven bars from end of Rondo.
   German: *Merrie England*, vs, p. 119, bar 5.

2. Beethoven: Violin Concerto, Rondo bar before A.
   German: *Merrie England*, vs, p. 21, bar 3.
   Kern: *Show Boat*, vs, p. 9, bar 12.
   Rodgers: *Carousel* vs, p. 176, bar 14.

3. J. Strauss: Waltz — *Wiener Blut*, m.s. bar 166.

4. Bruch: Violin Concerto, min. sc., p. 31, bar before A.
   Mozart: *Serenade for wood-wind*, Romance, bar 16.
   Sullivan: Overture, *The Pirates of Penzance*, vs, p. 5, bar 22.

5. Bruch: Violin Concerto, p. 42, 3 bars before G.
   Sullivan: *The Pirates of Penzance*, vs, p. 163, bar 4.
   Rossini: Overture, *L'Italiana in Algeri*, bar 18.

6. Sullivan: *Iolanthe*, vs, p. 165, bar 1.
   Kismet, vs, p. 68, bar 14.

7. Sullivan: *Mikado*, vs, p. 196, bar 5.
   Sullivan: *Princess Ida*, vs, p. 131, bar 15.

8. Sullivan: *Ruddigore*, vs, p. 44, bars 6 and 10.
   German: *Merrie England*, vs, p. 222, bar 3.
   Rodgers: *Carousel*, vs, p. 118, 5 bars from end.

9. German: *Merrie England*, vs, p. 25, bar 6.
   Rodgers: *Carousel*, vs, p. 117, bar 6.
   Sullivan: *The Gondoliers*, vs, p. 152, bar 6.
   Sullivan: *The Yeomen of the Guard*, vs, p. 103, bar 4.

When the pause covers two or more beats in the bar the routine of beating is as follows. Make the holding gesture on the last beat of the pause and then move straight into the next beat.

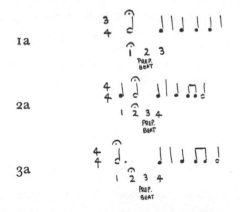

Some conductors give the holding gesture on the first beat in the pause (1a, 2a) or on the penultimate beat (3a), then use the final beat on the pause as a preparatory beat for continuing the music.

It is possible to give just one beat for a pause, no matter how many beats in the bar the pause covers, and then move on to the next positive beat of the bar. Intermediary beats are omitted.

1b $\qquad$ $\begin{smallmatrix}3\\4\end{smallmatrix}$ ♩ ♩ ♩ ♩ ♩

2b $\qquad$ $\begin{smallmatrix}4\\4\end{smallmatrix}$ ♩ ♩ ♩ ♩ ♩ ♩ ♩

3b $\qquad$ $\begin{smallmatrix}4\\4\end{smallmatrix}$ ♩ ♩ ♩ ♩ ♩ ♩

With professional players this is the best method, but when dealing with amateurs or mediocre professionals I have always found that the first method is the safest for two reasons. First the routine of 'moving on' is the same no matter how long the pause or on which beat or beats it falls. Second there are always some players who are not good at counting silent bars and unless the correct number of beats are shown in each bar they may become confused.

N.B. When beating through a pause that covers more than one beat the movements leading to the holding gesture should be small and negative.

2   The pause followed by a rest

If a pause is followed by a rest, the beat for the rest serves to cut off the pause as well as acting as a preparatory beat for the beat which follows and upon which the music continues.

3 *The pause on a rest*

If there is a pause on a rest the gesture known as the 'cut-off' has to be brought into use. This can be made in an upward or downward direction and to the left or right. The downward gesture is used, as a rule, as a finishing gesture at the end of a movement. Otherwise, when the music is to continue, the upward version is used.

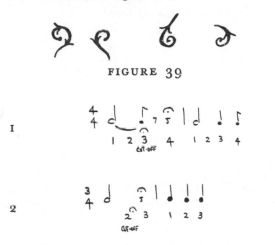

FIGURE 39

In example 1 the third beat is given as a cut-off in an upward direction at the end of which the baton is held quite still for the duration of the silent pause. Then the fourth beat is given in tempo, which serves as a preparatory beat for the first beat of the next bar.

In example 2 the minim* is cut off at the end of the second beat, afterwards the procedure being the same as for example 1.

The cut-off gesture is very necessary in places such as these, to ensure that all the players concerned are going to stop at precisely the same time and no one will add just that little bit extra, a fault known as 'tailing'.

*Half note.

In the following example a pause is made on part of a beat and this is the method of beating.

The third beat is made as a cut-off, then the pause is held; after which the third beat is repeated as a preparatory beat for the fourth beat of the bar.

The student must practise these cut-off gestures until they become second nature. The choice of moving to the left or right depends upon the beat which follows. If the cut-off is on the first beat of a bar in a four-beat bar, then the cut-off to the left is preferable, as this will bring the baton towards the field of beating for the next beat. A cut-off on the third beat in a four bar is better made to the right, as this follows the movement of the baton from left to right when making the next beat.

Finally when it comes to accompanying, especially singers with their little foibles in time keeping, it will be realised what a blessing this gesture can be!

6

Ebb and Flow—2

I   *Rallentando*

I T is easy to lay down a rough and ready rule for controlling a change of speed and that is, 'the slower the speed the larger the beat' and vice versa. Certainly the 'vice versa' can be accepted as a reasonable precept when making an *accelerando*, but be chary of 'the slower the larger' suggestion. All will agree that this is the obvious way to control a *rallentando* over a bar or two, or one that comes at the end of a phrase.

If however, the *rallentando* is spread over several bars it is impracticable to direct this by just increasing the size of the beat. It is by a combination of a gradual increase in the size of the beat coupled with a gradual decrease in the speed at which the baton travels from beat to beat that a long *rallentando* is controlled. It is also essential when 'slowing down' that a continuous movement of the baton is maintained and there should be no suggestion of a 'stop and go' progression, unless the music requires a *staccato* articulation. In such a case the baton has to stop momentarily at each point of beat.

First of all practise the short *rallentando* that occurs within a phrase and which is controlled by the size of the beat only.

MUSIC EXAMPLES

Weber: Overture, *Euryanthe*, bars 55–65. Poco
rall bars 59–60. Tempo bar 61.

Sullivan: *Mikado*, 'The Moon and I', final
phrase.

Sullivan: *The Gondoliers*, Gavotte. vs, p. 250,
bars 4–9.

Phillips: *The Rebel Maid*, vs, p. 142–6.

German: *Merrie England*, vs, p. 203. Duet Jill
and Raleigh.

Next practise the long *rallentandos* using the 'increase in
size and decrease in speed' method. Make certain that
there is a *gradual* slowing down and not a series of sudden
changes of speed as the *rallentando* progresses.

EXERCISES

2 *Ritenuto*

I hope that I will not offend by reminding the student that *ritenuto* is a sudden and not a gradual holding back of the speed. Bearing this in mind, it becomes evident that no preparation for the slower speed can be shown by the beat which immediately precedes it. Therefore the first bar of a *ritenuto*, no matter what the expression marks, must be beaten very decisively, so that there can be no doubt in the performer's mind as to the degree of the change in speed. With experience this can be done without altering the character of the playing.

It may not even be necessary to increase the size of the beat, but it will be very necessary to *define* the beats in a marked manner for the first bar of the *ritenuto*.

I have said 'decisively' and please bear in mind that a thrashing and flailing of the arms will not convey decision! It is at times like these that the conductor's eye can help; but more of that later.

EXERCISE

And now, having come to the end of the *rallentando* or *ritenuto*, *tempo primo* is marked in the score. Here it is not only possible, but essential, to give the last beat of the slower tempo in such a way that it will serve as a preparatory beat for the subsequent speed.

Symphony No. 8, first movement, Beethoven.
(*Boosey and Hawkes, Min. Score, bars* 41–44.)

On the third bar beat 1, 2 and 3 as a *ritenuto* and momentarily hold the baton still on 3. Then give a preparatory beat in the tempo of the next bar.

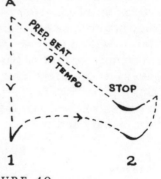

FIGURE 40

The second movement of Tchaikovsky's Fifth Symphony provides a comprehensive study in changes of speed.

3   *Accelerando*

'The faster the speed — the smaller the beat.' A reasonable precept as I said earlier, but not a complete solution for directing an *accelerando*. Once again we have to be prepared to combine the size of the beat with the speed of the baton. *Rallentando* in reverse, in fact.

Practise beating a steady *accelerando* in two, three and four in a bar, over a number of bars until the increase of speed is correctly controlled. The size of the beat must become smaller and the speed at which the baton moves becomes quicker. When the stage is reached where the field of beating can no longer be reduced the direction is by the increase of speed only. This is where a supple wrist is essential. A quick beat cannot be made satisfactorily if the forearm is used.

EXERCISE

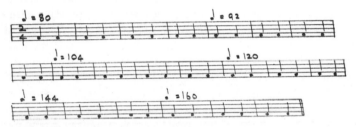

Repeat this exercise in ¾ and ⁴₄. When beating three in a bar, change gradually to one in a bar. When beating four in a bar change gradually to two in a bar.

MUSIC EXAMPLE

Symphony No. 5, Beethoven. Last movement.
(*Boosey and Hawkes min. score*, bars 350 to 361.)

This passage is a classic example of the need for a correctly graded *accelerando* if the music is to be given its rightful due.

4   *Changing the number of beats in the bar*

When an *accelerando* forms a link between a slow and a fast tempo it is often necessary to reduce the number of beats in the bar — from four to two or three to one.

MUSIC EXAMPLES

Weber: *Euryanthe*, Overture, Eulenburg Min.
　　Score, PP. 27 and 28.
Grieg: *Peer Gynt*, Suite No. 1, Fourth Move-
　　ment.

The safest way to change from four to two during an *accelerando* is to decide at which bar this is best done, mark it in the score 'in 2' and change the beat accordingly. Also see that this is marked in the orchestral parts and do not get carried away at performance and forget the change of beat. If you do, and there is a 'bad moment', the fault will be yours and yours alone. Orchestral players have every right to expect a conductor to beat the same way at performance as at rehearsal.

The change from three to one can be made in the same way or the transition can be shown by a gradual modification of the pattern of the beat. This is done by shortening the movement of the baton to the right for the second beat of the bar.

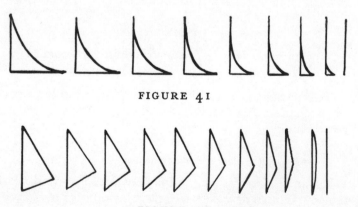

FIGURE 41

FIGURE 42

Rodgers: *Carousel*, Prologue.

Bizet: *L'Arlésienne*, Suite No. 1, Carillon.

Examples can also be found in the waltzes of
Johann Strauss.

5 *Piu Mosso*

The sudden increase of speed for a *piu mosso* can be directed
by a correspondingly sudden quickening of the beat. But it
is possible, if the difference between the two speeds is
sufficiently great, to offer a preparatory beat for the quicker
tempo. This is done in the same way as the return to tempo
was made in the example from Beethoven (Fig. 40).

6 *Changing from one tempo to another*

It is in the music of the romantic period that we first find
frequent changes of time signature within a movement
becoming normal practice. This progress in rhythmic patterns has continued and today changes can take place
every few bars or even every bar!

These extreme examples do not fall within the scope of
this primer, but the amateur conductor of the humblest of
operatic societies must be capable of indicating without
hesitation changes of time signature and speed within a
movement.

EXERCISE

Now let us turn to the finale of the first act of a popular operetta. *Iolanthe*, by Sullivan. Here is a plot of the time changes.

Moderato: Allegro Agitato: Piu Vivo: Andante Espressivo:

$\frac{4}{4}$ $\frac{4}{4}$ **¢** **C**

♩ = 69 ♩ = 144 ♩ = 96 ♩ = ♩ (♩ = 96)

Allegro: Allegretto: Allegro con brio: Recit.: A Tempo:

¢ $\frac{6}{8}$ **C** **C**

♩ = 104 ♩ = 76 ♩ = 144 ♩ = 144

Piu Vivo: Allegro Vivace: Moderato: Recit.: Allegro:

¢ $\frac{3}{4}$ **¢** **¢**

♩ = 92 ♩. = 72 ♩ = 88 ♩ = 100

Allegro Molto: Allegro Marziale.

$\frac{4}{4}$ (in 2) $\frac{2}{4}$

♩ = 116 ♩ = 112

When guiding the performers through such a sequence of time changes the conductor uses either the 'sudden change' method or the 'preparatory beat on the last beat of the old tempo' technique which we have discussed.

Here are the rhythmic patterns of the changes in this finale. The page numbers refer to the vocal score published by G. Schirmer.

PP. 93 and 94, vs.

Moderato   Allegro Agitato

Bar 2, pause on the first beat, then give the fourth beat in the new tempo, *Allegro Agitato*.

This fourth beat will act as a cut-off for the pause as well as a preparatory beat for the new tempo.

P. 95.

Allegro Agitato   Piu Vivo

The first bar is beaten four in a bar and let the fourth
beat lead into a marked down beat in the new tempo, *Alla
Breve* (two in a bar) and mark the accent on the second
beat with a firm unequivocal up beat. This will settle the
players in the new tempo.

P. 98.

          Piu Vivo   Andante Espressivo

The change from *piu vivo* to *andante espressivo* is helped
by the *rallentando* on the last bar of the *piu vivo*. Beat four in
bar 1 and plan the *rallentando* so that the last beat is in the
new tempo.

P. 101.

          Recitative   Allegro

The last four bars of the *Andante Espressivo* are a recitative accompanied by tremolo chords; one for each bar. All
such bars are beaten with a down beat only. This is the
normal procedure for conducting recitative, of which more
later. Give a down beat for bar 1, then watch the singer
and give a preparatory beat for the *allegro* (two in a bar) so
that the first beat of the new tempo synchronises with the
singer's word 'heart'.

PP. 101–102.

Allegro   Allegretto (in 2)

Cut off the second beat in bar one. Hold still for the silent pause, then give preparatory beat in the new tempo for the *Allegretto*.

P. 103.

Allegretto   Allegro con brio

In this case the second beat of bar 1 has to be given in strict time, therefore it cannot serve as a preparatory beat for the *allegro con brio*. This will be shown by the sudden emphatic down beat on the first beat of bar 2. (The 'piu mosso' routine.) All four beats in bar 2 will have to be very precise and any tendency of the orchestra to play *forte* will be checked with the left hand.

The change from *allegro* to *piu vivo* on P. 108 is done the same way as the change on P. 95. The *piu vivo* should be marked in the score ₵.

P. 116.

Piu Vivo   Allegro Vivace

The first two crotchets of the $\frac{3}{4}$ are part of the preceding phrase and are taken at the same tempo. I suggest that the first two or three bars of the *allegro vivace* are beaten three in a bar with, from bar 2 onwards, a strong down beat and small secondary beats which will diminish very quickly to leave a steady one in a bar beat. (See Figs. 41 and 42.)

The remaining changes of time signature in this finale should now present no problems.

It will be found that there are occasions when it is necessary to subdivide the beat in order that a change of tempo should be made cleanly by the players.

Overture, *Iolanthe*, P. 3.

Andante   Allegro Giocoso

This is a difficult change to bring off correctly if the last $\frac{3}{4}$ bar is beaten in three, for then there will have to be a sudden change of speed and time signature, over which the violins, who play the quavers, will stumble. If the second and third beat of the last $\frac{3}{4}$ bar are subdivided, it will be found that the last quaver in the $\frac{3}{4}$ becomes an exact preparatory beat for the $\frac{6}{8}$.

7

Colour and the Helping Hand

The character of the sound will reflect the character of the gesture.

NO matter how thoroughly the student has mastered the exercises in the previous chapters, with their aid he cannot indicate anything more than rhythm and speed, and an orchestra or choir performing under his direction will be lacking in expression; his beat, as yet, describes nothing more. The time has now come for solving the problems involved in defining dynamics, articulation and phrasing.

RIGHT HAND

1 *Dynamics*

A bold gesture should draw forth a bold sound; a quiet gesture — a quiet sound. So it would appear that a *forte* passage is conducted with large gestures and a *piano* passage with small ones. Whereas the application of this maxim holds good for many occasions it is not the only way of marking *forte* and *piano*; furthermore there are times when to use this method would be quite wrong.

Let us examine the 'Entrance and March of the Peers' in *Iolanthe*, P. 41 vs. The first nineteen bars should be marked *forte* with a *crescendo* on the bar before A. If the rule of the 'louder the larger' be applied, the first six bars will be directed with fairly bold gestures. This, however, is incorrect when one considers the number of players who are involved. There are only three, the drummer and the two trumpeters and a large beat will not only be superfluous but may fidget the players.

Here is the rhythmic pattern of the bars we are about to discuss.

Allegro Maestoso. **C**

At bar 1 look towards the drummer to make sure that he is ready and then give a strong but not a large down beat, followed by three small but precise beats, finishing with a crisp down beat on the first beat of the second bar.

Follow this with three neutral beats and repeat the process for bars 3 and 4.

Now direct the trumpets with more small but intense beats. At bar 7 follow a small crisp down beat with three bold beats directed to the orchestra in general. Each beat must be strongly marked at the point of the beat to ensure, not only good ensemble, but also that these chords are accented. From bar 12 onwards it is only the beats upon which the full orchestra enter that need to be strongly marked; the remaining beats in the bar just indicated as a guide. It is unnecessary to keep up the intensity of beating throughout for the sake of the trumpet players, who will be well in their stride by now and are probably no longer watching the conductor.

The *crescendo* before A is shown by three beats of increasing size and intensity which will lead to the minim chord at A. For this bar (20), and those of similar rhythm, do not emphasise the second beat in the bar. A bold 1, a small 2, then a bold 3 taken straight across the body to the right, is what is required. This is a typical example of what I said earlier about the sound reflecting the gesture, especially if the conductor, instead of giving the fourth beat as a crotchet beat, gives the half beat which coincides with the last quaver chord.

When beating the *tutti* chords from bar 12 onwards, do be very careful that, in spite of the emphasis required on each of these beats, the beat is shown in the correct part of the four in a bar pattern. For the chords on the third beat bring the baton straight across from left to right; for those on the second beat give a clear gesture to the left and good up beats for those on the fourth beat. Keep the intermediary beats small and negative in character, so that there is no possibility of some inattentive player mistaking the beat and entering in the wrong place. Very disconcerting for all concerned when this happens!

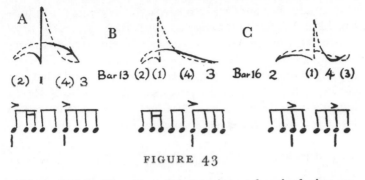

FIGURE 43

Now all this direction of dynamics and articulation *can* be done by the baton only, but here is where the left hand may, at long last, be brought into action. However, we will leave any discussion of the 'helping hand' for the moment and continue concentrating on the right hand only. In the meantime let us look at the problem of indicating *piano*.

A small beat close to the body is a very useful way of asking for a *piano*, so long as it can be seen by the players and is meticulously outlined. But here, once again, is a method which does not serve all cases. For example, take the opening of Schubert's 'Unfinished Symphony'. The beats should be small, but the baton should be held well away from the body, as it has to be seen by the 'cellos and basses, who are invariably way back on the platform.

One can never be dogmatic about the size of the beat to denote any particular dynamic, for the speed of the music has to be taken into consideration. It would be stupid to try and conduct an *adagio, pianissimo*, with very small gestures. At such a slow speed, and I am taking an extreme example in order to make my point, the baton must have some room to move in; it is therefore inevitable that the gestures cannot be as small as those suitable for indicating *pianissimo* in a quick movement. It is the manner in which a beat is made that defines the dynamics.

A gradual drawing in towards the body is an unmistakable indication of a *diminuendo* and always seems the most natural way of showing this change of dynamics. No matter how many players are concerned in this — it may be a few or the whole orchestra — this method can be used when the *diminuendo* is called for; the players are all, musically speaking, in their stride and so they need not watch the beat as intently as they would in an opening phrase.

2   *Articulation*

The different ways of articulating a passage of music, *legato, staccato, marcato, sostenuto* or even *tenuto* on one beat, are shown by the way in which the baton moves from beat to beat and how the point of the beat is defined.

Legato, according to my dictionary, means 'in a smooth, connected manner', and what else is needed to describe how to beat a passage marked thus? Yes, one thing. Without breaking the smoothness of the beat, make sure that each point of beat is clear. This is best done by a *slight* quickening of the movement of the baton as the point of beat is about to be given; but there must be no sharp movement which would probably result in an unwanted stress from the performers. This is a purely visual guide as to the divisions in time.

Irrespective of dynamics a *staccato* note is indicated by a sharp 'staccato' gesture, with the baton held quite still at the point of beat before moving to the next beat. This will show exactly what is wanted from the performers.

Example 1 is beaten with intense, but not large gestures.

In example 2 the gesture will still be *staccato* but no longer intense, only crisp and neat.

MUSIC EXAMPLES

Forte Staccato.
Glinka: *Russlan and Ludmilla,* Overture.
Sullivan: *Princess Ida,* Introduction.
Sullivan: *Princess Ida,* Finale Act 1, *Allegro marziale.*
Sullivan: *Patience,* Colonel's song, vs, p. 26.

Piano Staccato.
Rossini: *L'Italiana in Algeri,* Overture.
Beethoven: Symphony No. 8, *Allegretto scherzando.*
Sullivan: *Princess Ida,* Trio, vs, p. 53.
Sullivan: *Patience,* Bunthorne's song, vs, p. 55.

Marcato — marked; strongly accented; with much emphasis. What more can be said about this style of articulation when it is to be called for by a movement of the baton? The baton must keep moving between the beats as for *legato,* but each point of beat is shown with great emphasis.

MUSIC EXAMPLES

Beethoven: *Egmont,* Overture.
Bach: Brandenburg Concerto in G.
Weber: *Euryanthe,* Overture.
Schubert: Symphony in B minor. Second movement from N for 18 bars.
Sullivan: *Princess Ida,* Finale, Act 1, vs, p. 109, Full chorus.
Sullivan: *The Yeomen of the Guard,* Finale, Act 1, vs, p. 133.

Sostenuto, which we all know means sustained, is shown by a drawing out of the movement of the baton from beat to beat, but in doing this do not allow the music to drag in such passages.

MUSIC EXAMPLES

Mendelssohn: Symphony No. 3, *Adagio*.

Bizet: *L'Arlésienne*, Suite No. 1, *Adagietto*.

Sullivan: *The Yeomen of the Guard*, Act II, vs, p. 222, 'Oh day, etc'.

Sullivan: *The Yeomen of the Guard*, Recitative, Elsie, vs, p. 83.

Weber: *Der Freischütz*, Overture, Phil. Min. Score C.

Weber: *Euryanthe*, Overture, Eulenburg Score, bar 129, *Largo*.

Tenuto on a particular beat is shown by a slight drawing out or hold on the beat concerned.

A—LEGATO

The thickness of the lines in these diagrams denotes the degree of intensity in the movement of the baton.

B—STACCATO

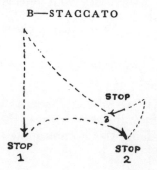

On each point of beat the baton stops on a downward movement. Were it to stop on an upward movement, this would indicate a pause or hold.

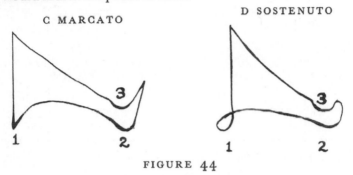

C MARCATO   D SOSTENUTO

FIGURE 44

LEFT HAND

The correct function of the left hand is to aid and not imitate the right hand. Nothing is more distracting in the concert hall than to have a conductor who is perpetually beating time with both hands. In the theatre, what with the different seating arrangement for the orchestra and the singers working on a higher level, there are times when duplication of the beat by the left hand is necessary.

1   *Dynamics*

All conductors have their own method of indicating light and shade with the left hand and it is noticeable that these gestures are based upon a simple rule.

For a forte the left hand is held well out from the body, palm upwards, in a gesture of appeal. Then if a *crescendo* is called for the arm is slowly raised until the peak of the *crescendo* is reached.

For a *piano* or *diminuendo* the arm is held, palm downwards or towards the players, and, for a *diminuendo*, brought slowly down and in towards the body. The sudden *piano* is shown by a quick downward movement of the left hand.

In carrying out these gestures any exaggerated crouch-
ing down for *piano* and springing up for the *fortes* are to be
shunned. I agree that it is inevitable that in directing
sudden or marked dynamic changes the stance of the conductor is bound to alter. It is perfectly natural when less
tone is wanted (and how difficult it can be to get a real
piano from some players and singers), that the conductor's
whole body will assume the attitude of 'Oh, please . . .
piano, piano'. But do not get carried away and disappear
behind the desk!

Conducting a *fortissimo* passage invariably results in an
upright stance and bold gestures from both hands, but
don't overdo things. No matter how great the tension,
emotion or volume of sound there is in the music, the beat
must remain clear and unmistakable and the more econo-
mical the gestures by the left hand the better.

2 *Phrasing*

Although nuance can be clearly indicated by an expressive
use of the baton as it moves from beat to beat, it is the left
hand that is able to help more readily in describing with a
free movement, completely void of any suggestion of time-
beating, the actual shape of the phrase.

When accents are called for, from either an individual
or the whole orchestra, the left hand is an invaluable aid,
especially if the left hand is used only on the beats in question.

Here is an example of a *tutti* chord which cannot be
directed without help from the left hand.

TUTTI

TYMP.

The left hand sustains the *tutti*, whilst the right hand cuts
off the tympani and then joins the left hand in completing
the *tutti* pause.

The left hand is always used to help the finish of a *tutti* sustained chord by making a replica of the right-hand cut-off gesture.

When there are two contrasting indications such as *legato* melody and *staccato* accompaniment, the left hand can be used to guide the melodic line with a free *legato* movement, whilst the right hand directs a *staccato* accompaniment. As a general rule it is better to conduct the *legato* melody and leave the *staccato* to the players concerned.

MUSIC EXAMPLES

Sullivan: *Cox and Box*, Serenade.

Mendelssohn: Symphony No. 3, *Adagio*.

Tchaikovsky: Piano Concerto No. 1, *Andantino semplice*.

Schubert: Symphony in B minor, Second movement.

Saint-Saens: 'Danse Macabre', 15 bars before B.

3   Cueing

The left hand is indispensable when it comes to giving cues. Admittedly individual players are sometimes best cued by a look from the conductor, but a section of the orchestra or a soloist or the chorus in a stage presentation, need a clear indication and this is given easiest by the left hand.

But first a warning. Do not get into the habit of perpetually cueing every entry. We have all seen conductors who appear to take a fiendish delight in giving every possible cue, not only with their left hand, but also with their baton. Players don't like this, because no good musician has to be told of every entry. Also this everlasting cueing often degenerates into an admonitory finger or baton being poked towards the player at the precise moment when he has to play. This is not very clever when you think it over.

When it is helpful to give a cue, first of all look towards the person concerned a few bars before the cue comes up and catch his eye. Then with a small preparatory gesture (Fig. 30 to the right) give him the beat upon which he must enter. As Sir Henry used to say, 'Catch his eye first, then bring him in'. This preliminary look is even more necessary when conducting for the stage. For your sake, as well as the singers, look first for unexpected things to happen on the stage that may require the conductor to make a slight adjustment in his beat.

It is sometimes better to ignore the preparatory gesture when dealing with a vocal ensemble, say a quintet. A quiet point to each singer on their cue is sufficient. If done properly these gestures cannot be seen by the audience and they are all that is required to help the singer enter with complete confidence.

For a big choral entry the gesture will have to be truly commanding if the desired result is to be achieved. Intensity of beat is not enough; size is needed as well.

4 *Warning*

A most useful function that only the left hand can perform is that of warning performers to keep an eye on the beat. This is a situation which all conductors have to cope with frequently; in particular when neutral beats are given which just mark the rest in the bar. See pp. 40 and 41.

This warning gesture can also be used to help correct a false entry by either a player or singer.

The above hints are only a few of the ways in which the left hand functions, for this is something which develops as the conductor becomes more experienced. The important thing to remember is that the left hand must never make a gesture unless there is a good reason for so doing. The more sparing the use of the left hand the more effective it becomes when it is used.

8

Accompanying

'TWO minds with but a single thought.' This is the ideal partnership when two people make music together. The accompanist at the piano who just trails along or who is too retiring is just as tiresome as he who tries to force his own ideas upon the soloist. Such performances are rarely heard in the recital hall today, but they are occasionally met with at an orchestral concert or in the theatre.

INSTRUMENTALISTS

We have all heard at some time or other a concerto in which there has been a complete lack of rapport between the soloist and conductor and so, instead of listening to one person's interpretation of a work we have had half of one and half of another. No way to present great music. Flexibility is the attribute of a mind of quality, and whenever a soloist is involved the conductor should approach their mutual task at least prepared to listen to the other chap's point of view.

It is possible for two great artists to work together in perfect harmony and what a joy it is for the audience. I recall many such occasions. I also recall many first appearances of young artists at the Proms under Sir Henry when, without imposing his will upon them unduly, he has helped them give of their best. I have often heard, also, Sir Thomas Beecham say to a soloist: 'My dear boy, I think *we* can improve on that. Don't you?'

The first step in preparing an accompaniment is for the conductor to have a piano rehearsal with the soloist. If he cannot play himself, then he must get someone else who can to be present. Now no matter how strong his views are on the work to be played, he must keep an open mind and be receptive to another musician's interpretation. He may even find it more mature than his own! He will then, having adjusted his outlook, be able to direct the *tuttis* so that they are presented as an integral part of the work and not mere interludes.

On the purely technical side of accompanying we must consider the problem of time lag. The conductor should be able to anticipate when a soloist is going to pass from one note to another and so move his baton just a fraction of a second in advance, so that the point of beat is reached simultaneously with the soloist. He should not rely upon his ear only to guide him, but watch as well.

All would-be conductors should take every opportunity of playing the piano for all kinds of soloists; string, wood-wind and brass, as well as singers. The soloists should stand where they can be seen by the accompanist, who must watch them closely. It will be found that there are quite clear visual signs connected with phrasing that will be in-valuable in getting a true ensemble. Watch the bow of the string player, the mouth of the wind player and the general physical bearing as well as the mouth of the singer; all will help.

To watch is a *must* when the soloist moves on after either a *tenuto* or a pause.

Let us take a brief glance at two well-known instrumen-tal works.

PIANO CONCERTO IN A MINOR. GRIEG
(*Eulenberg Edition*)

Bar 2. Obviously the soloist takes the beat from the conductor.

Four small neutral beats for the next four bars and wait for the last chord from the piano to be cut off before continuing.

Eighth bar after A. Beat with the soloist, left-hand gesture of warning for entry 'a tempo'.

Animato. Take the speed from the soloist. Give first and third beats only on the first bar and then continue in four.

At B cue oboe.

Piu Lento. Make sure that your tempo is that of the soloist when he enters four bars later. Avoid having to adjust the speed.

Fourth bar after C. Be sure that your second beat synchronises with the first of the triplet on the piano.

The entry at D is very tricky indeed. Listen to the octaves in the left hand and watch the soloist. Beat a neutral first beat in the bar and then move quickly on to the position of the fourth beat so as to be ready for a quick preparatory beat for the *Animato* at D.

Eight bars before E the soloist takes the beat from the conductor for the *arpeggi*.

In the last movement there are four orchestral entries which are very difficult to synchronise with the soloist. In each of these cases the orchestra enters at the end of a brilliant scale passage. I had occasion to discuss these entries with Sir Adrian Boult, whose sympathetic and impeccable accompanying is known the world over, and here is his solution to these problems.

The first one is at the commencement of the *poco animato* on page 65. It will not help if the conductor listens deliberately to every note in the preceding scale passage. All he should do is to listen for the four G sharps and on the fourth one give a preparatory beat for the orchestral chord at the beginning of the next bar.

At bar 3 of page 68 the same principle should be applied. Although there is no indication of a change of speed, this passage is invariably taken *poco meno mosso*. Give the preparatory beat on the third G sharp. There are some soloists who, by continuing this passage for a further octave, change this bar into two bars played in tempo. In such cases it is quite easy to lead the orchestra at the *tutti* entry at A.

On page 79 it is the low G sharp and the next one an octave higher that should be listened for.

At bar 5, page 91, there is a repetition of the passage on page 68.

The *Andante Maestoso* at K is a typical passage where the soloist plays under the baton of the conductor.

The above are a few hints to help over difficult places.

VIOLIN CONCERTO IN G MIN. BRUCH

(*Eulenberg Edition*)

Allegro Moderato

Bar 5. Beat four unobtrusive beats, giving crescendo with the left hand, and glance towards soloist for his entry at bar 6.

Six bars before B hold the speed steady, as nearly all violinists tend to slow down a little when playing these triple stops.

Seventeen bars after C, *stringendo poco a poco*, the conductor remembering from rehearsal the soloist's intention, can take charge here.

At F, having indicated the previous three bars with a quiet down beat on each bar, give another one for the first of this bar and then be ready for a quick fourth beat leading to the *Allegro Moderato*. Watch as well as listen to the soloist.

Adagio

Cue the soloist for his entry and then watch his bow. It is usual for this opening bar to be played with a full bow and so the speed of the movement can be gauged.

Before K, 1 bar, cut the violins off with the left hand and hold the 'cellos on with the right.

Finale

At 1 the soloist has sixteen bars of *arpeggi* as counterpoint to the first subject. Now some players, and good ones, too, are inclined to 'pull' such passages about (I suppose it could be called *rubato*), but don't try and follow. The conductor should take charge of these bars.

In short cadenzas, such as are to be found in this work, it is advisable to mark each bar with a neutral down beat. In a long cadenza it is only necessary to indicate the beats in the last two or three bars. But make certain that the number of bars you treat thus is noted in the orchestral parts.

VOCALISTS

Gilbert in one of his cutting moods, once wrote of a singer, 'Miss —— suffers from the quaint idea that it is necessary for her to breathe during her songs and complains that her costumes are too tight!' Any singer will tell you that there are conductors who sometimes regard the taking of a breath as 'a quaint idea' and are not helpful at such moments; in fact their beat is too tight.

Working with singers brings its own particular problems for the conductor. The first of these, breathing, has already been mentioned. The solution to this and other problems concerning phrasing, diction and the odd 'high note', suggests that all conductors, no matter how dreadful their voice, should study singing under a good teacher, then they can evaluate the difficulties that beset even the best of singers, and he who understands can help.

It is possible, albeit undesirable, to drive an orchestra rather than lead it, and still get a good result. But to try this method with singers is most unwise and frankly futile.

But let us return once more to the basic requirement of good accompanying, that of synchronising the orchestra with the soloist. I said earlier that it is helpful to watch as well as listen to an instrumentalist when accompanying. In the case of singers it is *essential* to watch them. By watching it is possible to tell in advance the progression of the phrase, as the formation of the mouth does not change simultaneously from one word to another, but always gives some kind of warning movement.

Written 'And so'   Sung 'A . . . ndso'

Try to follow this by ear and you'll invariably be late on the word 'so'. Watch the movement of the mouth and you will see the mouth close as the 'nd' of 'and' is sung. This movement acts as a visual 'preparatory beat' and it is then quite easy to synchronise the orchestra and singer on the word 'so'.

In addition the conductor will find it essential to be able to give the clearest indications of *tenuto* and *rubato*, as well as handle pauses with complete assurance.

The problems of phrasing and interpretation when working with singers will be discussed later.

Recitative

When accompanying recitative a free style of conducting is used. Unessential beats are omitted, for what the orchestra needs is a clear beat for each chord and nothing more.

TRIAL BY JURY*, Sullivan, P. 35, VS

Usher: 'Where is the Plaintiff?   Let her now be brought.

Oh An-ge - li - na   Come thou in-to

(ORCH.)   (ORCH.)

Court!   An-ge - li - na

(ORCH.)

Bars 5 to 7. Give three quick neutral down beats to mark the three silent bars. Bar 8 omit the first beat and give a down beat for each of the two successive chords.

The singer enters *after* and not with, the second chord. This is known as 'clearing the chord' and is frequently found in classical recitative. In this particular case the usher makes a step on each of these two chords, after which he sings.

Bars 9 and 10. Having given a down beat on bar 9, hold the baton still until it is time to beat the next two chords.

Do not beat the next four bars, but gather the orchestra with your eye and carry on normally at Q.

'H.M.S. PINAFORE', SULLIVAN, P. 28, VS

Bar 1. Neutral beat.

Bars 2 and 3. Down beats for each chord.

Bar 4. Four beats.

Bar 5. Beat first and second beat only.

Bar 6. Down beat only.

P. 29, bar 1. Four in the bar.

Bar 2. Down beat only and hold for duration of dotted minim.

*N.B. *Trial by Jury* and all Gilbert and Sullivan operas are from the editions of G. Schirmer.

Bar 3. Beat two and three only.

Bar 6 down beat only, then move to fourth position ready to beat.

Bar 7 in four. (First beat neutral.)

Bars 8 to 9 the same as 6 and 7.

Bar 10. Down beat only.

Bar 11. Neutral 1 and expressive 2 and 3.

Bar 12. Down beat for minim.

Bar 13. Neutral down beat; hold until chord on fourth beat which is directed with a firm gesture.

'MERRIE ENGLAND', GERMAN, p. 140, vs
(*Chappell & Co.*)

Bar 1. Down beat with left hand marking the *sf* chord.

Bars 3 and 4. Brisk four in a bar.

Bars 5 and 6. Accented one and two only, holding the second beat for duration of dotted minim.

Bar 7. Mark with a small neutral beat.

Bars 8 to 12. Two in a bar.

Bar 13. Down beat only.

Bar 14. Three in a bar.

'RUDDIGORE', SULLIVAN,
RECIT. AND ARIA, p. 66, vs

This recitative differs from those already referred to as it is a *Recitativo Stromentato*, or accompanied recitative. Although it is sung rhythmically, the speed varies according to the picture that the singer is describing. These changes are not marked, except the *Allegro Vivace*, where the time signature alters; they are left to the artist.

Bar 1. Beaten in six ($\flat$ = 116) with *poco accelerando* which continues through the first three beats of bar 2. The dotted crotchet is given a strong *sf* beat, followed by a cut-off for the quaver chord on the third bar. The flute is left to play the cadenza *ad lib*. I mention this so that there is no attempt at direction from the rostrum; it should be discussed and rehearsed, under the conductor's guidance, in private.

The fifth bar, *a tempo*, is played by two clarinets and it is very difficult to get a neat ensemble unless they are given something more than the usual up beat. The best thing to do is to beat, in tempo, a discreet '1 2' ($\downarrow$. = 88), on the last part of the flautist's minim pause. The flautist will take the second of these beats as his cut-off and the clarinets will then be able to enter with precision and play accordingly.

Mark the *sf* for wood-wind on the next bar with a sharp '1' followed by a less tense '2'.

Turn to the strings for the next two bars, which are played *pizzicato* with a good rise and fall in dynamics.

The triplet and quavers in bars 1 and 2 of page 67 are played on the tympani. Give a quiet beat for these and the next two bars. The chord is for strings *pizzicato*.

At bar 5 sustain the strings with the left hand while continuing to direct the tympanist.

The singer enters and sings *quasi parlando*, but rhythmically. After the phrase 'comfort me not' the mood is reflected by the bassoon, who plays the melodic phrase on the next two bars. Take these bars *poco rallentando*.

At the bar marked tremolo pick up the tempo and beat a strict two in a bar. Don't forget to cue the horns and bassoon, who play the chords after the words 'buzzes the bee'. A slight *rallentando* is effective on the last three bars of this section.

After the pause bring the singer in and continue with a brisk but *piano* beat ($\downarrow$ = 116) with a crescendo to the fifth bar. Mark this *sfz* very strongly and follow it with a quick *diminuendo* for the next bar and then give another *sfz*. On bar 9 of vs, p. 69 and for the next four bars the singer *must* take the beat from the conductor or the syncopation will not be correctly sung.

At bar 15 give a very expressive *piano legato* beat at a somewhat slower tempo, *andante con moto.*

The words 'That's all' are sung very pathetically, so reflect this mood when directing the strings in the two groups of chords which follow.

The $\frac{6}{8}$ movement, which is the aria, should be taken at ♩. = 60. A smooth *legato* beat of two in a bar takes the music up to bar 20 on page 70. Here, for the next four bars, the woodwinds take over from the strings, and the chords as gently articulated as those for the strings at bars 5 to 8 on page 71.

The woodwinds join the strings for the remainder of the aria.

Bars 11 and 12 are broadened slightly, but do not take them in six. If you do the orchestra will drag.

It is allowable for bar 14 to be sung *molto rallentando*, in which case it must be beaten in six, as the flute doubles the vocal line and, in a theatre pit, the flautist cannot always hear the singer. If he could, two or even one beat would suffice.

THE SINGER AND THE CONDUCTOR

In the case of the ill-informed singer, professional or amateur, there can sometimes be considerable misunderstanding as to the function of the conductor: 'After all, I'm the one who is singing, not him!' I wonder how often this has been said behind the conductor's back?

In the concert hall a good singer has every right to expect to be 'accompanied' when he or she is down to sing a couple of arias, but if a complete work is being given, *The Messiah* or the like, the conductor is there to direct and mould the whole as he thinks the composer intended it to be performed.

This is accepted, without question, by all good singers. I do not suggest, however, that the young conductor who is fortunate enough to be able to engage established soloists for his first *Messiah* starts off with the idea of showing them how it should be done. That would never do. Young musicians should always listen to the voice of experience.

But if the soloists are all amateurs, then the conductor can approach his work with the feeling of 'What I say goes'. This situation is unusual in the choral society, but is the general rule in the operatic society.

Unfortunately what a conductor wants and what he gets are two very different things. A performer can only give of his best within the limits of his technical equipment and, although the conductor's conception of how a part should be sung may be the ideal one, he will have to modify his demands if the singer just can't make it. Of course, sometimes the word 'can't' is used when really it should be 'won't'. Then it is up to the conductor to discuss and convince the unwilling one that 'Father knows best'. This may be easier said than done if he cannot offer a reasoned and intelligent argument in support of his views. If he has conscientiously prepared his work in advance he will have all his arguments ready; learning to deal with situations such as these is a very useful accomplishment.

As a final resort, in an extreme case, he can produce his trump card — 'Well, I'm the conductor and that is how it is going to be done', but avoid this if possible. Persuasion is by far the better method, because then the singer will willingly respond without any feeling of frustration.

With the willing singer of limited technique, tempo will have to be adjusted so that difficulties of articulation, both of notes and words, can be smoothed out. Phrasing also may have to be altered because of inadequate breath control.

Sometimes a radical alteration of the 'thought behind

the word' will be the only way round a difficulty. For instance in the *Pirates of Penzance*, in the duet in Act 2 between Frederic and Mabel, 'Stay, Fred'ric, stay', I heard a soprano with a charming lyric voice almost sing herself out by being too commanding in the first two pages (PP. 159–60). Although I prefer this section to be sung with real drama, I suggested that instead of 'commanding' Frederic, she 'appealed' to him. Doing it this way took all the strain off her voice and the resulting performance was not only well within her capabilities but was every bit as convincing.

It may be thought that the last few paragraphs do not have any direct bearing upon the technical aspect of the art of accompanying. Perhaps in the strictest sense this is true, but taking the broader view of accompanying, which is 'to keep company with', I am sure that they will offer some guidance as to how to get the best out of a performer, and that should be the primary consideration of him who directs.

9

The Conductor and the Stage

I T is natural and right for us musicians to concentrate the whole of our energies and skill to giving the best possible performance of any music that is placed in front of us. In the concert hall and recital room we are fortunate because there is nothing else to think about but the music, always the music.

What happens when we work in the opera house or theatre? In the former, although the stage (using the word in its broadest sense, including acting, costumes, décor, lighting and so on) is involved, the music still takes precedence over all else. In the theatre, where the music heard is of the operetta or 'musical' genre, the music is no longer the principal medium through which the story is unfolded, but an accessory. How, then, do we adjust our point of view when we enter the theatre and what exactly is implied by this 'accessory' business?

We shall have to start by examining the function of the music in examples from each of our three arenas. From the concert hall, the third movement, *poco allegretto*, of Brahms's Symphony in F; from the opera house the aria 'When I am laid in earth' from Purcell's *Dido and Aeneas* and from the theatre 'I'm goin' to wash that man right out of my hair' from *South Pacific* and 'Vilia' from the *Merry Widow*.

The Brahms has its own special message for all who hear

it. The performers will do everything in their power to translate into sound the composer's intentions when he put pen to paper. But what did the composer intend and are we sure that the music awakes in us a similar response? That is one of the imponderables of our rare and beautiful art. I have listened to many fine performances of this music which, incidentally, Sir Henry once described to me as 'the supreme example of absolute music', and at times I have heard a lingering sadness in the opening bars, at other times a tender happiness. This changing response on my part has occurred even when listening to the same performance; my favourite recording by Furtwängler! Response to 'absolute' music is bound to be subjective.

It is a different thing altogether when we sit in the opera house. Here there can be no doubt as to what the composer is expressing. In *Dido and Aeneas* Purcell says in terms of music what the poet is saying in words. But, important as the words are, the dominant medium of expression is the music. Even if the listener does not understand English, he should be fully aware of the dramatic content of the scene by listening to the music only.

In the theatre music is no longer the senior partner. Sullivan himself wrote to this effect in reference to the Savoy operas. 'It has hitherto been word setting. I might almost say syllable setting; for I have looked on the words as being of such importance that I have been continually keeping down the music in order that not one (word) should be lost. . . .' One has only to recall a few successes such as *The Mikado, The Merry Widow, Oklahoma!* and *My Fair Lady* to realise that the music was written for the story and not vice versa. The musical director can console himself for this unpalatable statement with the fact that being an 'accessory' does not imply that the music need not receive its full due in the way of an elegant and stylish performance. Quite the reverse: style in the performance of this type of music requires just as much and maybe a more highly developed sense of the *stage* than grand opera. Anyhow, in light opera a merely wonderful singer cannot 'get away with it' by just singing beautifully, as is sometimes the case in grand opera.

Let us take a quick look at the two examples from the theatre and imagine that we are hearing them for the first time, not sung, but played by an orchestra. The tune from *South Pacific* is a gay piece of nonsense and nothing more. When we hear it sung we realise that as a vehicle for expressing Nellie's feeling about 'that man', it is very good. In the other example, 'Vilia', we hear a typical Viennese sentimental melody, soothing to the ear, if you like that sort of tune, and nothing more. But hear it sung with impeccable style by Schwarzkopf and you will then be able to judge the music correctly and fairly. As Schwarzkopf said when being questioned about this kind of music, 'This music is difficult to sing, as not only must it be flawless, but it must appear effortless to give it the lightness and gaiety that are essential.'

THE CONDUCTOR'S RESPONSIBILITY

If the conductor of an operetta or a 'musical' is going to take his rightful place and not be just an 'accompanist', he will have to approach his work from an entirely fresh angle. He will have to learn to see things through the eye of the 'stage'. It is no good him thinking to himself 'What does the music express?' Instead it must be 'What is the dramatic content of the scene and what is the character saying?' When these two questions have been answered, and not before, then is the time to look at the musical setting which, if the composer knows his job, will illumine the scene in question.

Especially is this approach necessary when the lyric is

part of the narrative or just 'tells a story' which is free of any personal emotion. In *Merrie England* there is a song which Wilkin sings in which he tells the story of King Neptune and his court. The musical setting is quite charming of its kind, but, on its own, is of no significance. As a vehicle for the lyric it is excellent. Therefore, while insisting upon an immaculate musical performance, the conductor must not forget that it is the *words* that are of primary importance and a clear, intelligent delivery takes priority over all else.

Even when the music has a more definite character, such as the stately 'O Peaceful England' from the same operetta, it is not enough to allow the singer, even if she has the voice of the century and technique to match, to just stand on the stage and pour forth a stream of beautiful sound. We must see and hear Queen Elizabeth speaking to her people. Any conductor who is satisfied with less is either lackadaisical or has no understanding of what a stage presentation should be. If this song is included as an item in the concert hall, what I have said about 'just singing' still holds good. No matter how elegant the phrasing or majestic the voice, there is not enough in the music itself for this to suffice. There must be the words and the thought behind the words. It has been suggested that this matter of 'getting the number over' is the responsibility of the stage director. I disagree wholeheartedly with this and say that it is the musical director who is responsible for the 'sung word'. I will enlarge upon this later in the chapter.

MOVEMENT

This leads us to another aspect of the stage performance and one which can put a considerable strain upon the relations between the musical and stage directors. This possible bone of contention is to do with 'movement'.

On the stage a performer must express himself not only by voice but with his whole body, and in so doing there comes a time when the natural result of a thought is a movement. Now these moves are not left to the performer and the inspiration of the moment, but are carefully planned and plotted by the stage director. Unfortunately it happens at times that the stage director directing his first 'musical' wants the performers to move at places most inconvenient for the singers as well as the conductor. The former will not be madly enthusiastic to have to cross the stage as the climax of a phrase approaches, neither will the conductor approve of a singer having to turn or move to a position where, at some crucial moment, he cannot be aware of the beat.

I hope that you noticed the word *aware*. I did not say *look at* the beat, for this is quite unforgivable in a stage performance. The singer should, if he is standing sideways on to the conductor, be aware of the beat out of the corner of his eye, or, if he is facing downstage and needs guidance, he should look at a spot about twelve inches over the conductor's head. Then he will see the beat quite clearly. Never should the singers *look* at the conductor, for if they do they are no longer 'in' the stage picture. By directing attention to the conductor they are no longer in character or in the scene; they are, for the moment, translated into singers in costume. I have spent a lot of my time in the pit and I complain bitterly if a singer makes a habit of looking me straight in the eye at a performance. Any idea that the chorus should deliberately look at the beat, as they would in the concert hall, must be discarded. They have to be so well rehearsed that they will be able to sing as required when only a few are in a position to be aware of the beat. It is only in extremely difficult choral ensembles such as are to be found in the Rossini operas that the whole chorus must be so placed on the stage that they are all singing to the front and so can all be aware of the beat.

But to return to this problem of movement when singing, either of the singer himself or of other actors present, when he has an important solo. Providing the movement is done with a reason, to underline a thought or emotion, neither the conductor nor the performer will find it distracting, but if it is a case of movement for movement's sake, then it cannot be allowed. Not a hand should be raised by anyone on the stage without a reason. Any modification of movement where a few principals are concerned is usually agreed upon without any great argument. But when the chorus is involved in an important scene, then sometimes, once more if the stage director is new to this kind of production, things are inclined to run amok and the focus of attention blurred. Only recently I saw a production in which one great scene was, in my opinion, ruined, because the chorus was not allowed to stand and sing for more than a few beats without fidgeting about in meaningless business. This was carried to such a pitch that the brilliance of the musical setting and the wit of the lyric were completely lost.

There are occasions when the musical director should put his foot down and be able to give sound 'stage' reasons as to why the movement must be curtailed. Although in one's heart of hearts the reason may be 'because it spoils the music', this argument will not convince or influence the stage director, who needs to be tackled with his own weapons. It is not always necessary for a chorus to be rushing around the stage in order that the scene should look animated, and neither does having to stay on one spot and sing mean that the soloist need stand like a stuffed dummy and 'just sing'. There must be a lively reaction to the drama shown by each individual, otherwise the scene means nothing. The musical and stage directors have to consult and come to an agreement, before the first rehearsal, over this important question of movement on the stage.

THE CAST

The other vital matter, also to be agreed upon by these two in advance, is how each character is to be played, and that, of course, includes the singing, for when speaking or singing a performer retains his stage character.

The stage director is apt, understandably, to disregard the musical side of the play when he visualises his characters and the general style of the production. On the other hand, the musical director is apt to use just the vocal score for his study. It is correct for him to do this with a grand opera or a classic comic opera by Mozart or Rossini, for the music quite definitely gives an unmistakable delineation of character and mood. Think of 'Una voce poco fa', for instance. Here in each witty and elegant turn of musical phrase can be seen reflected a facet of that disturbing, delightful and a slightly alarming person, Rosina. This cannot be said of well-known songs in equally well-known operettas and 'musicals'; so to study the music is not enough. The script must be studied as well.

It may appear to some that the duties of the two directors are clearly definable and that each has his own 'departmental duties' to perform, more or less independent of each other; the musical director being responsible for the singing and orchestral playing and the stage director for the business or acting. To accept this premise as a foundation upon which to build a production is disastrous, for the work of the two directors either overlaps or is interdependent for the greater part of the time the curtain is up.

An operetta or 'musical' is founded upon a plot which is broken down into scenes which are played by the characters in either word or song. It is the musical director's job to see that, when singing, the cast remain in character and the dramatic content of the scene is made clear and maintained.

This is the way in which a conductor should organise his preliminary study. First study the cast list and form a rough idea of the relative importance of each part, a general idea of the characters and the type and range of voice needed. Then read the script, after which a careful study is made of the vocal score with the intention of getting a general idea of the musical setting.

Now is the time to go into consultation with the stage director; get from him his views on the characters, how each part should be played, and then how each scene should be played — broad or light comedy, sentimental, satirical and so on. Then comes the tricky part; seeing how the stage director's views match up with the musical director's. It is most unlikely that there will be complete agreement throughout, and if the production is to be successful any differences must be resolved at this point and not left until rehearsals have started. The stage director will have to be persuaded to appreciate the importance and significance of the music, and realise that he cannot build up a character which would be at variance with the musical setting of the numbers that this character will be singing. On the other hand, the musical director will have to be prepared, if necessary, to modify his demands from the musical angle, in the interest of obtaining the best possible all-round performance. Only when complete agreement has been reached should the musical director start coaching the singers. For then he will be able to coach them intelligently and not just teach them 'words and music', leaving the characterisation to the stage director. *Characterisation in operetta and 'musicals' is as much the responsibility of the musical as the stage director.*

The same routine applies in training the chorus, with

the result that from the first business call they will sing in character and so play their part in unfolding the drama. When a complete cast is coached in this way much time is saved at business calls, and the stage director has the pleasure of working with singers who have an intelligent foundation upon which to build their performance.

10

In the Pit

GENERAL

TO all of us who have spent long periods working in the theatre have come times when we longed to be back in the comparative cloistered calm of the concert hall. Work in the theatre can be very exciting and give to all concerned a tremendous feeling of achievement when the performance has been a good one; it is, however, work which brings its own particular difficulties.

There is always something 'going on' on the stage which does not come under the heading of music, but is of vital importance to the production and has to be taken into consideration by the conductor. I have already mentioned movement and today it appears to be the fashion in some quarters that if the cast isn't moving the scenery is!

How, then, does this change from one arena to another affect the conductor? Conducting is still conducting no matter where one is working, and what are these additional difficulties?

Let us begin by looking at stage production as a whole. Although it may not be noticed by the average member of the audience, one of the most important features of any stage production is the general flow of tempo throughout the whole of the performance. When music is concerned the conductor has the responsibility of maintaining this flow, and this includes variation of tempo that was agreed upon by him and the stage director at rehearsals. Surely this is nothing to be unduly worried about, for, as I have said, everything has been thoroughly rehearsed beforehand. Of course it has, but when it comes to the performance the conductor will have to be extra alert and sensitive to the relationship of the musical numbers to their immediate context and, in order that a scene which is partially dialogue and partially music may be presented as a complete unit and not in two separate parts, he may have to modify the tempo of the music slightly in order that it shall match the 'speed' of the playing of the spoken part. This is a tricky thing to put into words, but I will try to explain what I mean.

Let us imagine that we are in the pit and a comedy scene is being played, at the climax of which the cast break into song. Now this is where the matter of speed comes in. It may be that in response to a warm audience the playing may be just a little gayer in mood than is usual, so the music should be picked up with a similar brightening of the mood so that this spirit of extra gaiety which has suddenly appeared is continued without a break. As a general rule there can be no speeding up or slowing down when a scene moves from speech to song.

Here are two examples which illustrate this rule very clearly. In the first only one character is involved; Don Alhambra, the Grand Inquisitor in *The Gondoliers*. The Don has been talking to the Duke and Duchess and then he continues with the following: 'A doubt? Oh dear no. . . . Listen, and I'll tell you all about it.' He speaks with unhurried authority and great dignity and, in order that his delivery in song should be consistent with his mode of speech, the music must be taken at a speed whereby he can make his statement in song with precisely the same dignity with which he speaks. The other example of a perfect transition from speech to song in which the mood of the scene, as well as the mode of speech, is continued when singing is in the film *Carmen Jones*; the scene in the bar when Carmen Jones is being persuaded to leave for Chicago. The argument is started in speech and suddenly one is aware that all concerned are no longer talking but singing. I have watched this film several times in order to pin-point the exact spot where the change is made, and I am still not sure about it. This, however, is not the point I wish to make; what is apposite is the fact that the speed of speech and song is consistent.

But how about scenes where the mood has to be changed completely when the music starts. Isn't the conductor allowed a free hand then? Sometimes yes; sometimes no. If there is no foreshadowing of a sudden change of mood, say as in *The Yeomen of the Guard* when in the middle of a comedy scene the bell is heard presaging the execution scene, then the conductor is in sole charge of the new tempo. On other occasions the change in mood may be foreshadowed by a remark spoken by the character who is responsible for the new mood. In such a case as this the conductor should be able to foresee the way in which this character is going to continue, and so start the music accordingly. There is an interesting example of this need for sensitivity in *The Mikado*, Act II. Ko Ko and Katisha have had a scene of high comedy at the climax of which Ko Ko threatens to commit suicide if Katisha will not marry him. Katisha, in a fury, says: 'Go to. Who knows as well as I, that no one ever yet died of a broken heart.' Ko Ko then changes the whole atmosphere of the scene by saying in a quiet voice: 'You know not what you say: listen.' Then is heard the introduction to the Tit Willow song. Now the mood in which the introduction is to be played can be gleaned from the way in which Ko Ko speaks his words. I have conducted this work many times. Usually these words are spoken with quiet sincerity, but sometimes the same actor unwittingly will speak them with a hint of drama, at other times as if annoyed. If I have been conducting I have felt it only right to direct the introductory bars with a similar feeling in mind. The conductor must be able to carry on in music the thought in the actor's mind in circumstances such as these.

No matter how thoroughly a work has been rehearsed and how firm the directors have been in their intentions, when it comes to a performance there will always be human variability and there has to be firm but *sympathetic* guidance by the conductor.

PARTICULAR

The detailed problems of working in the pit are the same as those in the concert hall, with a few additional ones thrown in just to make life interesting.

First of all the seating of the orchestra. No longer do you have a large orchestra facing you in full view, but a smaller number of players, if you have as many as thirty you are jolly lucky, disposed mainly on each side of you with only one or two immediately in front. Several of them, unless watched carefully, will also be hiding behind large music stands. This matter of stands is a nuisance in some theatres, so make sure, well in advance, that those provided can be adjusted so that the players can see and be seen.

Before I go any further I will enumerate the four classic complaints which are made by one or the other of the players at every first rehearsal. They are: one, 'I haven't got enough room'; two, 'I can't see the beat'; three, 'I'm in a draught', and four 'There's a light shining in my eyes'. What can be done about these complaints? Well, your guess is as good as mine.

When planning your seating try and keep the percussion and bass near to each other and do not, as is so frequently done, place them on either side of the pit. If you do, and sometimes there is no alternative, the rhythmic foundation of the orchestra is likely to be shaky; these players should be able to hear one another. I have given some specimen plans in the appendix. Finally the conductor should be on a rostrum sufficiently high for his beat to be seen by the orchestra, but not so high that they have to strain their necks upwards, and for the stage to be aware of the beat without obviously looking down.

It is not possible to have the orchestra under your eye the whole time in the theatre, not only because of the way in which they are seated, but because it is the stage which needs watching so carefully. Singers, taken as a whole, are not noted for their sense of rhythm and, apart from having to 'act', they cannot always hear what is going on in the pit. Therefore for the conductor to devote the whole of his attention to the orchestra for any length of time is fraught with danger. He has to keep a watchful eye on the stage, not because the singers have to be 'conducted' the whole of the time, but in order to maintain his grip upon the performance as a whole. Although there are places where a strict control has to be exercised upon soloists and chorus, it is surprising how much difficult music can be handled by well-trained singers without any marked direction on the part of the conductor. The same goes for the orchestra, except that where this is concerned much depends upon the quality of the players and the amount of rehearsal they have had.

There are bound to be prolonged periods when conducting has to be done on two levels: one, the lower, for the orchestra, and the other, well up, for the stage. When this is necessary the conductor may even have to resort to 'two-handed' conducting, with the left hand duplicating the movements of the right hand. Such occasions do not frequently occur. As a rule it is quite sufficient for the left hand to mark the rhythm and articulation without having to beat time.

It is not possible to offer any hard and fast rule as to where the field of beat for the right hand should habitually be. Sometimes a fairly high position which will mean that it is in vision for both stage and orchestra; at other times the field of beat for the orchestra may have to be on such a low level that it is out of sight to those on the stage. Every theatre pit has its own difficulties and the conductor has to make on-the-spot adjustments to ensure that his direction will be clear to all. It is desirable however, that the principle of the correct use of each hand, as described in the opening chapters, be adhered to in the pit as far as possible.

In order to conduct operetta efficiently, the conductor has to keep a constant watch on everything that is going on, and this means that he remembers where everybody should be on the stage at any particular moment. He will have to watch entrances of principals as well as their musical entries. Nothing is more disconcerting, and I speak from experience, than, having been occupied with the orchestra, I have been unable to check that Miss X has made her entrance, then giving a quick glance up to give her her cue, no Miss X! Whether the left or right hand, or both, are being used for directing the stage, do not be misled by seeing the performers spread out in such a wide space that you start giving a much larger beat than normal. It is the decisive beat which keeps things moving in the correct way. Mind you, there will be occasions when a strong choral entry is called for, and where the beat will have to be correspondingly bold.

Cueing of singers is done in much the same way as when cueing the individual instrumentalists on the orchestra.

The preliminary glance followed by the invitation to enter.

Mis-entries

What is to be done when a singer makes a wrong entry? If the singer enters a beat late, then the conductor must give a 'hold everything' gesture to the orchestra and give a firm cue to the singer to wake up and start. If the entry is a beat early then all that needs to be done is to quicken the beat for the next bar or so and catch up with the offender. Sometimes a singer will enter too soon at the beginning of a song. A safety measure against this contingency is always to have the orchestral parts marked 'voice' at the appropriate bar. Then if there is a wrong entry the players can jump ahead with the singer.

Dynamics

In ensembles for the whole company a very close watch should be kept upon the chorus, who do at times, in their enthusiasm, sing so loudly as to drown the solo lines. The response to indications of dynamics lies in good training at music calls. It is infuriating when a body of singers, and principals are as great offenders in this respect as choristers, will not respond correctly to a request for *diminuendo* or *pianissimo*. It will be noticed however, that they are always delighted to sing loudly without even being asked to do so.

Movement

I mentioned 'movement' in the previous chapter without going into details as to how this may bring problems to the conductor. There is first of all, the normal walking from one position on the stage to another, which does not cause any trouble to either singer or conductor. Then there is the concerted movement by a number of people making either a grand entrance or exit, when they have to move either realistically (walk or run) or rhythmically to the music and, in each case, have to sing at the same time. Now, such large-scale movements can make the conductor tear his hair with rage if the singers get out of time, for it is often very difficult indeed to bring them back on to the beat. It is usually wisest to adjust the accompaniment to the singers, so that the audience will hear nothing wrong. But do not omit to have the offenders on the mat before the next performance, and when you have finished your scolding turn your attention to the reason for the mishap. In the case of the entry with realistic movement the cause is invariably aural inattention to the introductory music. In the case of the entry with rhythmic movement, ninety-nine times out of a hundred the root of the matter lies in insufficient rehearsal of the steps to which they move. In fact, they sing out of time because they move out of time.

Beware the dance step which has to be done whilst the chorus are singing an appropriately bright number. Now no matter how tempted the conductor is to smarten things up, he must remember these movements and avoid taking the music at such a speed that what should be a neat formal movement becomes a mad scramble.

Then there is the 'song and dance' number. Once more the tempo must suit both singing and dancing. Any possible diversion of opinion between the two directors will have to be resolved before rehearsals start. It is no good, if the singers are going to have to do the dancing, to allow a vigorous or complicated dance to be arranged, for then the singing is bound to suffer. Of course, the ideal thing is to have a group of dancers who can perform the movement leaving the singing to the chorus. It is amazing, though, what can be accomplished given enough rehearsal and the determination to succeed. So do not dismiss as impossible the stage director's pet idea without giving it a fair trial.

BEING HELPFUL

As well as directing the musical side of the performance, it is up to the conductor to be as helpful as possible to all concerned, so that they can give of their best. At times this can be done by giving way very slightly to artists in the matter of tempo or, on the other hand, it may be better to hold them firmly to the beat if they are showing signs of running away in a difficult number. Only experience can tell a conductor which to do and when, and more often than not it is best to hold the artist to the tempo which was established at rehearsal.

In certain circumstances the artist can safely be left to get on with the performance, especially when the 'big aria' is being sung, and the conductor can give all his attention to providing a worthy accompaniment.

Then there are the places where the timing of the music is linked with stage business. Dealing with this is again something which comes with experience, so that while helping the artist the conductor avoids any break in the flow of the music or performance.

This timing of business and music can best be shown by looking at one or two examples where, if the timing is not correct, the performance is bound to suffer.

'THE PIRATES OF PENZANCE',
ACT II, p. 159

Here we have a duet which is in three clearly defined tempi and moods. The first section is sung *allegro agitato*, during which Mabel appeals to Frederic to stay with her, but he says this is impossible as 'duty calls'. At the end of this section there is a pause during which time Frederic sits and Mabel sits at his feet before singing the next section, 'Ah, leave me not to pine alone'. This is marked *andante* and the two singers must not only be allowed sufficient time to take up their new positions, but also to settle down. So it is advisable to make a *ritenuto* on the last two bars of the first section which will reflect musically the action on the stage, as well as decreasing the tension of the two lovers. If this *ritenuto* is omitted and the pause cut short, there is a jerky change of mood which will not help Mabel when she continues singing. Again, at the end of this *andante* section, the chord which starts the recitative on page 163, must not be played too soon. Allow a little time before Frederic continues. Give him time to think before he sings 'In 1840, etc'.

'H.M.S. PINAFORE'

In this opera there is a splendid example of the need for the singer and conductor to synchronise the timing. Act I, page 62. The introduction to this duet is marked *allegro con brio*: it should be marked *allegro furioso*, for that is the mood in which Josephine sings. It is also the mood in which she sweeps across the stage after her indignant reply to Ralph's declaration of love. So to make the transition from speech to song correctly, Josephine's move across the stage must start with the first chord of the music.

If the picture in vision and sound is to be complete and the whole flow of production smooth, then music and business have to be considered as complementary. A performance must always be looked at in the round and not from one particular angle.

11

Style

STYLE is the hall-mark of a good performance, whether the work in question is a symphony, grand opera, operetta or a 'musical'.

Style is defined in the Oxford Dictionary as 'the manner of expression characteristic of a period'. If in a performance the style is wrong, the author's or composer's intentions will be obscured, and the audience will sense that something is wrong, but will not know the reason. I will enlarge upon this subject of 'style', only in relation to the types of works which are performed by amateur operatic societies; operettas, musical comedies and 'musicals'. These cover a wide range and include the elegant and witty Gilbert and Sullivan comic operas, the Edward German excursions into the English countryside, Edwardian musical comedies, the Ivor Novello package tours to Ruritania, and moderns such as *Oklahoma!*, *Annie Get Your Gun* and so on. There are also European importations from the works of Offenbach, Lehar, Messager, Strauss, to mention a few of the well-known composers.

I have, over the past few years, seen a varied assortment of amateur performances, some of which have been extremely good, others not so good, and a few frankly awful. The singing was usually good, sometimes very good indeed, and so was the acting; the weak spot in some of even the best performances was the general style of presentation.

'Style' is not to be confined to one aspect only of a performance; it must be evident throughout the whole — in acting, singing, costume, décor and make-up.

How does one set about deciding what is the correct style needed for a true presentation of a work? A question which is as important to the musical, as it is to the stage director. Not only the period of the work but the work itself has to be taken into consideration. What is it that the authors have written? Is it light or broad comedy, satire or sentiment, burlesque or parody?

The question of period is answered easily enough; if the date is not given on the title-page there is sure to be something in the dialogue that fixes the date of the action beyond question. To arrive at the correct answer as to what the authors have written is rather more difficult and entails a close study of the libretto and score. Rather than theorise upon this I will take some examples of the various types, analyse them and show how *I* arrive at a decision.

'PATIENCE'

Period: 'Greenery-Yallery', 1880-90

Chief protagonists: the two idyllic poets and the Dragoons. On the distaff side are the love-sick maidens and the down-to-earth milkmaid. The plot hinges upon the exposure of the affectations and insincerity of the two poets. The sentimental vapourings of the maidens with their Grecian poses, typical of the cult of aestheticism so popular in the Wilde–Swinburne period, form the background against which the plot is unfolded. The music is charming, elegant and witty. Sullivan at his best providing a delightful mirror in which Gilbert's intentions are admirably reflected.

This work is obviously a satire upon the aesthetic movement of the day and is accordingly to be played and sung with a corresponding elegance and a delicate underlining of the satire. Played too broadly it loses its bite.

'THE PIRATES OF PENZANCE'
Period: Victorian

The protagonists are Frederic, the 'Slave of Duty', the Pirate King and Major-General Stanley, aided and abetted by the Sergeant of the Police. The ladies are Mabel and her sisters and Ruth. The crux of the story is Frederic's devotion to duty, come what may. Fun is poked at the Pirates, the Police and the Major-General. The music is a parody of the Italian grand opera of the period.

Gilbert calls his work a 'new and melo-dramatic opera' and, even without this guide, it would be difficult to reach any other conclusion. The work is, of course, a burlesque and therefore should be played a 'little larger than life'. The singing must be sincere and in the grand operatic manner if it is to come over as an amusing parody and not an anaemic imitation of Italian opera. Care must be taken to avoid an exaggerated broadening of the performances. It is by pointing the lines, both spoken and sung, that the humour is correctly underlined, and to point is not to broaden.

'MERRIE ENGLAND'
Period: Elizabethan

This is an historical novelette of the court of Queen Elizabeth the First. A romance with the usual ingredients of love, jealousy, humour and a bit of patriotism thrown in. The music is well written and tuneful and suits the 'romantic' atmosphere.

There is no hidden meaning to be read into this work; it

is not satirical, neither is it burlesque or parody. It is just a story of well-known historical figures reacting normally to the situation in which they find themselves. The style of performance is therefore one of absolute realism. I admit that there is little similarity apparent between the stage characters of Elizabeth, Raleigh and Essex and those of history, nevertheless every effort must be made to present these three with some semblance of truth. Elizabeth is not just another contralto; this red-headed virago was a great queen and acted as such. Raleigh was not a sentimental tenor, but a great Englishman. So are the lesser folk in the work real people who play and sing with the uninhibited warmth and cheerfulness of the true countryman. Without this contrast of court and commoner the performance will be a flat one.

THE EDWARDIAN MUSICAL COMEDIES

These works, of which *The Geisha*, *Floradora* and *The Quaker Girl* are typical examples, should be always produced as period pieces, the period in this case being that of Edwardian days. Any approach towards present-day realism is not to be encouraged, as the structure of the plays and the music are too fragile for such treatment. Whilst a gay artificiality in playing and singing is the ideal to strive for, there may be no tongue-in-the-cheek attitude, for this would come over as insincerity. The characters are not real people but prototypes drawn from a world of make believe, a cloud-cuckoo land, that has little relation with reality, and so the performance is better free from any hint of deep feeling.

A comparison between the Salvation Army Lass in *The Belle of New York* and the one in *Guys and Dolls* illustrates my point. The former is a charming leading lady in costume, the latter a very human young lady.

THE IVOR NOVELLO ROMANCES

Ivor Novello drew upon the world of fantasy for his plots and characters who inevitably became involved in a grand passion. The music is undoubtedly lush and a 'grand opera' performance would be too much for the listener, but there must be great warmth and conviction in the singing.

THE EUROPEAN SCHOOL

It is very difficult for the Anglo-Saxon to imitate either the French or the Viennese style of acting and singing without which the works of these composers will lack the inherent gaiety and lilt, and will become earth-bound. So, if any of these operettas are contemplated I advise that the directors study them in conjunction with a good recording of a native company.

THE MODERN MUSICALS

For the past twenty-five years at least all the best 'musicals' have been American, for, with the advent of *Oklahoma!* a new development of the musical was made manifest. The book was taken from a fine play, *Green Grow the Lilacs*, in which ordinary, everyday folk were portrayed, and this had its influence on the music, which in turn became far more than just a collection of gay, tuneful and exhilarating numbers, as it had always been from the early days of Irving Berlin and Cole Porter. *Carousel* from Molnar's *Liliom* followed and a host of others. A book on trade-union troubles in the garment trade became *The Pajama Game*; an acid satire on the diplomatic world was seen in *Call me Madam*; the New York folk opera *Guys and Dolls* and finally the shattering *West Side Story*. No longer does the stage present figures from some world of fantasy, but instead people are seen whom one could meet in real life. Yes, even in *Guys and Dolls*, for I have met these types myself on 42nd Street.

Broadly speaking the style in the singing of such works is one of vitality and honesty. There is, however, a danger to avoid when it comes to the performing of the musical items. In this day of modern communications all the popular numbers from a successful musical are served up on radio, television and on LPs, in many varied forms from traditional to modern jazz, or sung by 'pop' singers each in their own inimitable manner, so the listener subconsciously absorbs a composite version of these numbers which bears little or no relation to the original, for both words and music are distorted. When the amateur productions are in preparation these erroneous impressions are likely to influence the singers, who, imagining that they are doing the right thing, may offer a lively but inaccurate version of what the composer wrote.

Another thing to avoid is the attitude of mind that regards modern musicals as being written solely in the dance idiom. Modern dance forms are used in the same way as polkas, galops and the ubiquitous waltz were used in earlier works. I have picked at random the score of *South Pacific*, and on looking through it I find, apart from the waltz, only three numbers in true modern dance rhythm. The remainder are straight numbers to be sung as such. The dance numbers should also be sung as the composer wrote them and not in a free style. A free style may be acceptable coming from an established artist with an individual style, but the finest performers adhere strictly to 'what the man wrote'. Hence the beautiful style throughout their work. To revert to the 'straight' number, listen to a recording of the Soliloquy from *Carousel* and note how accurately, as well as feelingly, Gordon McRae sings.

When conducting the dance numbers just keep a clear

springy two or four in a bar; do not try to emulate any of the showmen you may have seen at some time or other, and be very careful to keep a good balance between stage and orchestra. This latter may be easier said than done, for some musicals are very heavily scored. The brass and saxophones are the offenders, in particular the former, so if in doubt mark the brass parts 'muted'. The 'hush', 'cup', as well as the straight mute, can all be of great help.

But to return to the performers, who can only give to the audience according to what they themselves have absorbed of the work. Therefore they must understand clearly what the authors have in mind and how they wish their intentions to be presented. If the performers' studies have been solely confined to 'words and music', the audience will not find their offerings very thrilling.

The world of operettas, musical comedies and musicals call for a wide range of styles on the part of the performers and the most careful guidance in translating them on the part of the stage and musical directors.

12

Homework

IT has been said many times that there are two kinds of conductors, one with the score in his head, the other with his head in his score. In practice every conductor should start off, whenever he has a new work to direct, by having his head buried in the score in private, so that by the time rehearsals start he has the score in his head.

Sir Henry was insistent that all work should be thoroughly prepared before the first rehearsal and would take no excuse for this not being done. 'Don't tell me you didn't have time; you must make time. You're not going to stand up there and waste everybody's time while you get to know the score; it's an insult to the players.' No matter what the work in question is, symphony, choral work, grand opera or operetta, there is a great amount of preparation to be done at home. I am assuming that the conductor has read his score through, probably played it on the piano or listened to recordings of it, so that he is familiar with the music. Then, with conducting in view, he gets down to really studying the score.

First of all comes the question of 'How many beats in the bar?' He must take into consideration the rhythmic impulse as well as the speed of the music, make his decision, mark it in the score and stick to it.

MUSIC EXAMPLES

Iolanthe, vs, p. 106, bars 5, 6, 7 in 2; bar 8 in 4;
bars 9, 10, 11 in 2; bar 12 and onwards in 4.
p. 108, bar 13 in 2. *Piu vivo* in 2.

Merrie England, vs, p. 237, 1 in a bar; bars 15,
16 in 3; bars 17 to 20 in 1; bars 21, 22 in 3;
bar 23, etc., in 1.

Princess Ida, vs, p. 92, change from 4 to 2 in a
bar (♩ = ♪) on bar 6 or 7.

Next he has to check up on the ebb and flow and see if
any *ritenutos* or *rallentandos* call for a subdivision of the beat;
if so, mark the places. Check any pauses and make a note
of those which are followed by a caesura and any which
carry straight on.

Then come such matters as bowing, phrasing, nuance,
balance, articulation and so on.

Let us take the first movement of Schubert's B Minor
Symphony and look at some of the points to note.

Bar 1. Start on a down bow for this bar and the second.

Bar 3. Up bow.

Bar 9. Violins *pp* off the strings.

Bar 13. Violins *pp* on the strings.

Bar 20. Note the *fz* followed by *fp decresc.* Don't settle
for *fp subito*.

Bar 29. *fz* followed by *fp* ⇒.

Bars 37–40. Watch balance of bassoons and horns.

Bar 41. Watch balance of clarinets and violas.

Bar 43. Celli to play with a true *legato* and do not allow
any deviation from *pp*. So often is the phrase heard thus:

Bar 68. *fz* ⇒ then *crescendo* on bars 70–71.

Bar 74. Up bow for *legato* phrases.

Bar 78. Down bow and clean *staccato*.

Bar 133. Correct balance between alternate chords for brass and wood-wind.

Bar 176. As much bow as possible for every semi-quaver* and played near the bridge.

Bar 184. Watch rhythm ♩. ♪♪. ♪♪. ♪ Horns, trumpets, oboe and tympani.

Bar 187. True *staccato* and not *martellato*.

Bar 202. First of grace notes played *on* the beat.

Bar 204. *fp* ══ and strings ♫ ♩ p.

Bar 209. Watch strings ♫ | ♩ up bows. Clarinets and bassoons *molto legato*.

> In the tutti passages make sure that 𝅘𝅥𝅲's are played as semi-quavers and not *tremolo* which is shown thus 𝅘𝅥𝅲.
> Bow the string parts throughout, otherwise the tone and ensemble will suffer.

A comparison of the published score with the photographic facsimile of the original score issued by the Vienna Gesellschaft der Musikfreunde will bring to light two glaring discrepancies in the first movement.

In bar 109 Schubert continued the pedal B in octaves played by the first horn and second bassoon. In all printed editions the dissonance caused by the sustained B has been avoided by giving the horns an F sharp and the second bassoon a C sharp. A similar alteration is made in bar 327. This deliberate alteration of the composer's intention cannot be justified, for the composer has written this passage three times (twice in the full score and once in a rough draft) in precisely the same way.

Another matter for conjecture is that of the sign for an accent > and that for a diminuendo ══. Schubert did not always make it clear exactly what he intended. I will

*Sixteenth note.

quote only one instance where the printed score gives rise to a doubt.

In the last movement fourteen bars before the end the wood-wind and horns are marked with an accent thus > and the violins with a diminuendo thus ══. In the facsimile these signs appear to be identical and it is not unreasonable to regard them both as signs implying a diminuendo. There are other cases of ambiguity. There is a most interesting article to be found in the *Musical Times* for March 1954, in which Adam Carse discusses this whole matter.

N.B. Always make certain that the full score is the same edition as the orchestral parts. If it is not it may be that, whereas the score is marked alphabetically, the parts may be marked numerically, and that will mean that it is impossible to rehearse, as instructions cannot be given when a section or some particular bars have to be repeated.

If it is a choral work or operetta that is being prepared, leave the orchestral side until later and turn to the vocal score and first of all check the phrasing. If there is none, which is more often than not, then phrasing and breath marks must be added. The latter may have to be modified to suit the individual soloist, but do not tolerate the 'breath every two bars' method that some singers will use if not checked. Without careful phrasing of all the vocal parts there can be no hope of a polished performance.

Before orchestral rehearsals commence a check will have to be made to make sure that the phrasing for any wind instrument that is doubling the solo line is the same. In the wood-wind parts of the Gilbert and Sullivan operas no phrasing is marked, and unless care is taken the instrumental and vocal phrasing will be at variance. A model of phrasing for wood-wind and soloists can be found in any of Puccini's scores or those of French composers, especially

Massenet. These scores will well repay studying on this account alone.

A musician is apt, when studying a vocal work on his own, to concentrate upon the *music* and tend to neglect the words. This is a great mistake, for no matter what the work is, good diction is vital to the performance. In the past two weeks I have heard performances of Rossini's *Comte d'Ory* and Elgar's *Gerontius* and in both cases the diction of both soloists and chorus was beyond reproach. Musically speaking both performances were superb and the feeling and conviction with which the words were sung, from the gay nonsense of Rossini to the deeply religious experience in the Elgar, gave a sense of completeness not always evident when choral forces are employed. So the words must be studied as carefully as the music. Clear diction is something but not everything; intelligent delivery of the words must be the aim. The conductor cannot afford to neglect this side of singing, it is just as important as beautiful tone and intonation. It is not enough for the stage director to be the only one to mention this vital matter of diction; the musical director must be as insistent in demanding a high standard in this respect.

Where 'character' actors are concerned it is wise to make certain that they are consistent if they use dialect in their dialogue, for then they must sing with the same dialect. I have known it happen that they forget and drop into standard English. This sounds silly!

Once music rehearsals are under way the conductor will have to turn his mind to preparing the orchestral accompaniment. If it is a choral work that is in rehearsal, things should be fairly straightforward, as full scores are available and the orchestra is usually up to strength. So the accompaniment is prepared as for a symphonic work. Should it be a work for the stage, then things can be very different. If the conductor is lucky he will have a full complement of players and needs only to make the normal check on the lines that I have indicated earlier. There is one snag, however; there will be no full score to study. Just a vocal score with the orchestration indicated thus: *strgs. only — ww — brass sus.* and so on. This is not a great help when it comes to rehearsing; the only thing to do is to study the individual orchestral parts. Make a note of any particularly tricky passage and for the rest of the work rely upon your ear. This can be most tiresome at times and the question is always being asked: 'Why can't we have, at least, a properly cued in vocal score to work from?'

I suggest that the orchestral parts are marked in *pencil* showing the number of beats in a bar, together with any subdivision or sudden change of tempo if there appears to be any likelihood of a misunderstanding. This is only a routine job, but one which can save a lot of rehearsal time.

If finances won't allow a full orchestra to be engaged, then the conductor's work becomes much more complicated. First he must check to see if any important solo melodic phrases are cued in for another instrument of the same family; for instance, is a solo for flute written in as an alternative phrase for the clarinet or oboe? If this is not the case, then something has to be done about it or this important phrase will be missing entirely. A similar thing may occur in the brass and horn parts when notes, important to the harmony, are not cued in for alternative instruments. If the parts are correctly cued, then all that has to be done is to indicate when the part proper is to be played and when to switch to the cues. Once more mark such places in *pencil*. If the parts are not cued, then copy the important phrases and attach them to the appropriate part. Attach, please, do not 'stick in', or there will be trouble with the publishers when the parts are returned.

An excellent exercise for the young conductor, and one that will teach him a lot, should he be working with a small society and a correspondingly small group of orchestral players, is to re-score the accompaniment for the players at his disposal, always checking first that in so doing he is not infringing copyright. Perhaps he may only have two pianos, and here, once more, why not arrange the music properly. Of course if you engage two first-class professional pianists they can, as a rule, make it up as they go along, but if your players are amateurs, don't risk it.

One more word of advice. If you have a pianist in the orchestra who is playing from the vocal score, do not allow him to do more than provide a firm rhythmic accompaniment. This is the correct function of the orchestral pianist, so keep him to it and don't allow any frills.

I cannot emphasise too strongly how important it is for a musical director to prepare his work thoroughly in advance. It is not enough to have the final goal in mind; he must have his course mapped out down to the smallest detail, knowing just where difficulties are going to be encountered and how they can best be dealt with. Then his direction, from the very earliest rehearsal, will be free from any hesitancy, no time will be wasted and he will gain the respect and confidence of all who work under him.

13

Rehearsals

A DULL rehearsal is a waste of time. All rehearsals should be in the nature of a voyage of discovery; discovery of fresh delights in the work being rehearsed as well as discovery of hitherto unsuspected capabilities in the performers themselves.

Although I have in mind work with amateur groups, this holds good for professional groups as well. I have been present at many a rehearsal of a standard symphony (referred to by the players as 'an old war horse') under a great conductor and have come away with memories of newly discovered beauty in a work which I thought I knew by heart, as well as having heard a fine orchestra excel itself in performance.

But now down to earth, and let us think of the many rehearsals that lie ahead of the conductor of an amateur society about to tackle an operetta or musical.

First come the 'words and music' calls for the chorus, when all that one aims for is the right notes in the right time and the words that go with them. These calls can be a dreary chore if handled wrongly. It is no good expecting to get an intelligent response if one works on the principle of just hammering in the notes and words by mechanical repetition. *Never* start rehearsing a new piece of music without putting the singers in the picture first. Explain who they are, what they are going to sing and why. This last is very important. Awaken their interest as potential performers and let them see what is the ultimate goal. Only when this is done is it time to get down to the business of rehearsing. Even at the end of the first rehearsal, when they may have only a hazy idea of the couple of numbers or so that they have been trying to sing, have a straight run through with no stopping. Then show them where improvements are to be made and how in time, what is now something of a shambles, will become a very important part of the production.

At subsequent rehearsals get them really interested in blending their voices, make them listen to each other as they sing, show them how exhilarating it is to sing with real rhythm and not just plod along at so many beats in a bar. Then, when the time is ripe to get down to singing in real character, you should have some good material on which to work.

If during these early rehearsals the chorus has a really difficult number to learn (fortunately they are met with very rarely) do not take it up to speed until there is every chance of it being a reasonably good effort. In this way you can avoid getting the singers unduly worried about the number, and this will help later performances. Nothing is so fatal as allowing your singers to get a 'thing' about any particular number, for if they do something is sure to go wrong.

As well as rehearsing the chorus, the conductor has also been having music calls with the principals at which he has coached them on much the same lines as those for the chorus, and by now they should be ready to come to full music calls in which special attention is being given to any scenes which include the whole company. At these rehearsals make sure that the importance of the inter-reaction between principals and chorus is fully understood, so that the chorus do not regard themselves as so much background. Tell them that they are just as important as the principals and don't be afraid to say this in front of the principals either; it won't do them any harm!

When final music calls, prior to business calls, are held make a great point of intelligent singing. Get the 'thought behind the words' firmly impressed upon the singers, for they do not always remember that it is not so much 'what' a person says as what they think when they say it! It will help to clarify this last remark if one thinks of the many ways in which a simple request such as 'Come here' can be made — commandingly — appealingly — with despair or happiness and so on.

At the first business calls do not be disheartened to find that all your work has apparently been forgotten. This is inevitable, but do not let this state of affairs go on too long. When it appears that at last the singers know where they are supposed to be on the stage and have a fair idea of what they are supposed to be doing, step in and see that the music is given its rightful due.

As the great day approaches arrange to have a purely music call with the company and make them express in song the full dramatic content of the work as it has been rehearsed by both musical and stage directors. Such a rehearsal will pay big dividends at the next full business call.

Finally, do not keep all your inspiration for the moment when the house lights are lowered and the curtain is raised; be generous and hand some out at rehearsals too.

14

The Great Night

ONE of the most important duties of an orchestral player is that of tuning his instrument correctly. At rehearsals the conductor is able to check this himself, but when it comes to a performance the responsibility for correct tuning lies with the leader.*

It is sometimes more difficult to tune correctly in a theatre pit than on the concert platform, owing to the seating of the players and, unless the leader is quite firm in calling for quiet when the time comes, the A from the oboe cannot be heard clearly.

It is sometimes necessary to remind inexperienced oboe players that before a correct A can be given the instrument must have been warmed-up for a few minutes. In fact, all *good* wood-wind and brass players do this in the band room as a matter of course, but there may be the odd player who cannot be bothered. My only comment in such a case is that he must be *made* to bother. One badly tuned instrument can wreck the intonation of a complete section, especially if that section is wood-wind or brass.

And now, the orchestra having tuned up, the audience are waiting for the performance to begin. If it is a concert, then there is the inevitable hush on the part of the players that heralds the arrival of the conductor. Speaking as a

*Concertmaster.

member of many an audience, I feel that this is part of the performance and not just a necessary preliminary. Of course, in the concert hall there is not that exciting moment we experience in the theatre with the lowering of the house lights. This is the moment that the theatre audience has been waiting for and don't let it be spoilt by some thoughtless member of the orchestra continuing to twiddle away on his instrument. With the lowering of the house lights there must be silence in the pit, and then when the conductor enters he can take his bow and start the overture without delay.

When, at the end of the interval, the bell sounds for the orchestra to re-enter the pit, it is up to the leader to see that they do so at once and re-tune their instruments. This tuning should be carried out as carefully as the one before the performance. The leader must see to this and allow no perfunctory tuning.

At the end of the performance no one may leave the pit until the final curtain call has been taken, the house lights brought up and the conductor has left.

At performances of modern musicals it is usual for the orchestra to play one or two of the popular hits from the show whilst the audience is leaving. And very pleasant, too. But don't be inveigled by an enthusiastic stage director into adopting this habit when one of the classical operettas has been performed. I heard this once at a performance of a Gilbert and Sullivan opera and it was very out of place. When the curtain falls at the end of such an opera be satisfied with that.

Coda

IN order 'to conduct' are we, as my dictionary tells me, 'to direct, manage, govern, control' or shall we accept this meaning 'to lead the way'? I think it is the best one to accept; to lead the company on the way to fulfilling not only the author's intentions, but their own capabilities as individuals as well as part of the whole. We shall find that in leading the way, be it through a symphony, mass or operetta, all unknowingly the performers will accept our direction, management and control.

Where concerted music is concerned there has to be someone in charge and that someone is the conductor. His place is at the front leading, not at the back driving.

ORCHESTRA SEATING PLANS
FOR THEATRES

PLAN A

The disadvantage of this plan is the separation of bass and percussion.

PLAN B

A good plan for an orchestra of this size. The cello, bass and percussion are all within earshot of each other. "Rep." (repetiteur) refers to the assistant concertmaster; the "leader" to the concert-master.

PLAN C

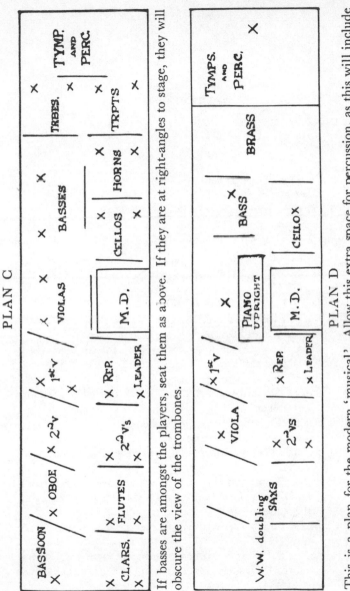

If basses are amongst the players, seat them as above. If they are at right-angles to stage, they will obscure the view of the trombones.

PLAN D

This is a plan for the modern 'musical'. Allow this extra space for percussion, as this will include vibraphone, xylophone, etc. etc.

SULLIVAN

'Iolanthe', Finale, Act I

Vocal score G. Schirmer.
Recordings on Decca and H.M.V.
The pages refer to those in the vocal score.

Moderato $\frac{4}{4}$

P. 89. Bar 1. An expressive *legato* beat using small gestures
directed towards cello and bassoon. Watch rhythm
♩.♫♫.♩ etc.

Bar 2. Bring in violins with L.H. *sempre p.*

Bar 7. Direct 2nd violins and viola *espressivo* ◁▷
over 7th and 8th bars.

Bar 8. Beat 1st and 3rd beats with quiet 4th beat which
will lead to

Bar 9. *Staccato* beats *p.*

Bar 11. Down beat only. Cut off the dotted minim and
cue singer.

Bar 12. Cut off gesture on 4th beat.

Bar 16. Neutral down beat only.

Bar 17. Watch singer and synchronise 1st beat with
voice.

P. 90. Bar 3. Cut off chord with upward gesture. Cue clarinets
and chorus. One hand directs the clarinets, the other
the stage.

Bars 7 and 8. With the L.H. lead oboe and indicate
nuance.

Bar 9. R.H. gives quiet but decisive beat for the ww
chord. L.H. cues singer on 4th beat. This also acts as
cut-off for the oboe.

P. 92.   Bar 1. R.H. directed to orchestra. L.H. cuts off chorus and cues principals.

Bar. 2. R.H. joins L.H. in directing singers; quiet *legato* gestures.

Bar 4. Bring in strings with L.H.

Conduct the whole of this ensemble with very *legato* gestures in order to prevent any jerky singing that this rhythmic pattern tends to bring about.

P. 93.   Bar 5. One beat only with upward sustaining gesture. Cut-off for chord followed by short caesura. Then give preparatory beat *ff* in new tempo for

Allegro agitato $\frac{4}{4}$

P. 94.   Bar 1. Vigorous *ff* beats, not large ones, directed to the violins.

Bar 2. L.H. cue singer. R.H. accent 1st and 3rd beats for *tutti* chords.

Bar 3. 2nd beat upwards to the right and hold the baton still. Watch singer and give preparatory beat to synchronise with 'Oh'. L.H. held still with warning gesture.

Bar 4. Small *p* gestures. 2nd and 4th beats almost omitted. L.H. is brought down on the 1st beat and gives indication of *p*.

Bar 11. Pause on cut-off on 3rd beat. Give small up beat on 'my'.

Bar 12. Small neutral beat on 1 and then crisp beats *f*.

P. 95.   Bar 2. Cue chorus L.H.

Bar 4. Strong 4th beat.

Bar 5. Hold semibreve with L.H. Strong beats with R.H.

Piu vivo ₵

Bar 6. Very strong direction to cellos and basses. Give accented up beat on 2.

Bar 8. Cue violas and give accented 2nd beat.

Bar 10. Cue 2nd violins.

Bar 12. Cue singer and 1st violins, who enter at the same time. Small *p* gestures, two in a bar.

P. 97.   Bar 11. *f* up beat for ww, continue *marcato*.

Bar 14. 2nd beat *sostenuto*, directed to strings.

P. 98.   Bar 1. Cue singer L.H.

Bar 8. Subdivide and synchronise with singer.

Andante espressivo ₵

Bar 9. *p legato*. Cue singer.

P. 99.   Bar 3. On 2nd beat cue clarinets.

Bar 5. Cue and direct chorus with L.H.

P. 100.   Bar 11. Cue flute solo. It is sufficient to do this with the eye only.

Bar 13. Smart *fp* down beat only for this and each of the next two bars.

P. 101.   Bar 3. Down beat and hold baton on the rebound ready to give preparatory up beat on 'give my'.

Allegro ₵

Bar 4. Firm two in a bar. The dynamics of the first four bars are as follows.

Indicate these with baton and L.H.

Bar 8. 2nd beat *p espressivo e crescendo* to

Bar 12. *f marcato*.

Bar 15. Cut-off on second beat; hold baton still for pause, then give preparatory beat in tempo for

Allegretto ⁶⁄₈

P. 102.   Bar 1. Quiet non-expressive gestures. Cue singer, flute and clarinet.

Bar 15. This bar is usually sung *ritenuto*. Subdivide the second beat. Sometimes it is advisable to beat six in the bar in order to maintain a better control over the singer.

P. 103.   Bar 1. As for previous bar.

Bar 2. Quiet down beat and wait for singer.

Allegro con brio ₵

Bar 6. Mark the change of tempo with brisk decisive beats. L.H. controls dynamics.

P. 104.   Bar 9. Quiet down beat, then *f* directed to the whole orchestra. Very firm cue to chorus with L.H.

P. 105. Bar 6. Lean on 1st and 3rd beats.

Bar 8. Accent on 2nd beat. Cue chorus.

P. 106. Bar 1. Cut off chorus with L.H.

Bars 5 to 7. Down beats only.

Bars 8 and 9. Two in a bar; cue chorus.

Bars 10 and 11. Down beats only.

Bar 12. Brisk four in a bar.

P. 107. Bar 2. Direct a *diminuendo* with L.H.

Bar 3. Catch chorus eyes and cue. Light *staccato* beats with R.H.

Bars 6 and 8. Direct phrasing with L.H.

P. 108. Bars 12 and 13. Slight *accelerando* changing to two in a bar at bar 13.

Piu vivo ₵

Bar 14. *Sempre p*, two in a bar. During this section keep a watch on the soloists and cue chorus with L.H.

P. 112. Bars 2 and 3. Big *crescendo* aided by L.H. Last crotchet on bar 4 should be marked *fz* and directed with an accented up beat.

Bar 5. *Subito p* gesture with L.H.

P. 113. Bar 11. Start *crescendo* and continue for four bars, then *diminuendo* to *pp*.

P. 114. Bar 5. Precise *pp staccato* beats for orchestra. L.H. controls chorus.

P. 115. Bar 6. *Crescendo molto*; still *staccato* beats.

P. 116. Bars 5 to 8. *Forte non-legato* beats.

Allegro vivace ¾

Bar 8. Beat one, two (♩ = ♪) and allow short caesura before cueing singer. Continue one in a bar *p* non-expressive.

P. 117. Bar 15. Change to *staccato* beat. Keep an eye on the chorus. It may be necessary to give them a duplicate beat with L.H.

P. 118. Bar 14. It is advisable to change to a small three in a bar for a few bars at this point, to ensure that the string playing is rhythmically accurate.

P. 119. Bar 6. *Sostenuto* beat.

Bar 13. Subdivide in order to get accent on second crotchet.

Bar 17. As for bar 13, then continue one in a bar. Control singers with L.H. Make sure that the chorus do not overpower the principals and do *not* allow any *accelerando*.

P. 122. Bar 7. Two *p* detached beats in a bar. This section should be marked *alla breve*.

P. 127. Bar 9. Cue oboe for melodic phrase.

P. 128. Bar 6. This and the next three phrases are for brass only. Beat four in a bar. Watch the balance between trombones and trumpets.

P. 129. Bar 4. Warn with L.H. and give two small neutral beats on one, two, then positive beats on three and four.

Bar 8. Two beats.

Allegro ₵

Bar 12. Two *p* beats in the bar.

₵

P. 132. Bars 1 to 8. Give 1st and 4th beats only for five bars. Then down beat only.

Allegro molto

Bar 9. Down beat *ff* and continue two in a bar. Cue chorus and keep strict tempo to the end of the section.

Allegro marziale $\frac{2}{4}$

P. 133. Bar 7, etc. Brisk military two in a bar. The vocal parts are doubled in the orchestra, so make sure that both singing and playing are exact. Watch the *p* in the A flat section on P. 137 and again on P. 138, bar 5, where the wood-wind double the voices. On P. 140 in the *fortissimo* passage do not let the brass force their tone. On P. 141 see that the strings, as well as the wood-wind, observe the semiquaver rests.

Build this section to a brilliant finish.

BIZET

L'Arlésienne Suite I

Prelude. Edition Eulenburg

P. I. Bar 1. Small 1st and 2nd beats with wrist only, then bold 3rd and 4th beats, *ff staccato*, using forearm.

Bars 2 and 3. *Tenuto* beat on 1st beat for ♩♪♩. Continue full *staccato* to end of page 2.

P. 3. Direct wind quintet with *pp legato* beats. Only small gestures are needed. The L.H. indicates dynamics and phrasing.

P. 4. Bars 1 to 4. *Animez*. Direct *pp staccato* beats to the whole orchestra. L.H. controls the *crescendo*, helped by increase of intensity of beats.

Bar 5. Bold 1st, 2nd and 3rd beats. 4th beat *pp subito*, L.H. indicates sudden change of dynamics.

P. 6. Steady increase in intensity of gestures finishing with *ff* 1st and 2nd beat at bar 4, page 7.

Before continuing with the next section, *Andantino*, allow a short 'breath mark'.

P. 8. *p legato* beats directed towards the cellos and horns. Give each beat with a slight 'click', which will help the bassoons in playing their counterpoint. This is very necessary in bars 7 and 15, where the first bassoon has a trill.

On the last bar give a *fortissimo* rebound on the 2nd beat directed to the whole orchestra to prepare for the Tempo 1. Give the 3rd beat with a bold gesture right across the body. The L.H. can help, too.

P. 11.   *pp subito* in bar 1. L.H. gesture to help indicate this with the R.H. suddenly changing to small beats.

N.B. The *crescendo* does not start until bar 4 and continues for four and a half bars.

P. 13.   Bar 1. Bold 1st and 2nd beat. L.H. cuts off the full orchestra and R.H. directs horns and cornets *ff*.

Bar 3. L.H. directs brass semibreves in *molto diminuendo*. R.H., aided by eye, leads flute, clarinets and bassoons.

Bar 5. L.H. cuts off horns and then joins R.H. for cut-off of wood-wind at bar 6.

Bar 7. Precise *pp* beats. L.H. cut-off gesture on 2nd and 4th beats.

Bar 8. Down beat only.

Bar 9. R. and L.H. indicate the finish of the chord. *N.B.* Give strings time to mute their instruments.

P. 14.   *Andante Molto.* ♩ = 63.

Bar 1. Small gestures directed to violins. L.H. aiding in marking the *ppp*.

Bar 2. Look towards saxophone and cue with L.H.

Bar 3. Include 2nd clarinet and indicate nuance.

Bar 4. R.H. continues directing strings. L.H. gives cut-off for semiquaver rest and continues leading the two soloists.

Bar 10. R.H. takes over directing saxophone and clarinet.

P. 15.   Bar 1. Lead flutes and cor anglais with L.H. indicating

Bar 5. L.H. controls *crescendo* in strings and cor anglais whilst R.H. directs saxophone and clarinet. Sharp *sf* on second beat for the saxophone.

Bar 6. Cue violas with eye.

Bar 7. Mark the *diminuendo* clearly.

Bar 8. Indicate *ppp* with L.H. Lead harp with precise but small beats. Cut off wood-wind with R.H. on 2nd beat. L.H. takes off strings on 3rd beat.

P. 16.   Bar 1. L.H. leads wood-wind and horn.

Bar 2. R.H. leads harp.

Bar 4. R.H. leads harp and violins.

Bar 6. The metronome mark ♩ = 76 is not consistent
with the indication *Etwas Langsamer* (a little slower).
From this bar to bar number 10 direct strings with
R.H. Lead wood-wind with L.H. The gestures to be
molto espressivo, but giving precise beats throughout
for the benefit of the 2nd violins and cellos. Control
the dynamics as the composer has marked.

P. 17.   Bar 1. Decisive cut-off with L.H. for the wood-wind
and vigorous sharp gesture for the syncopation for
the violins.

Bar 2. *Molto espressivo* gestures for strings. L.H. guiding
the phrasing. Mark each 1st and 3rd beat with a discreet but clear 'click' for the sake of the horns,
cornets and bassoons.

P. 18.   Bar 5. Direct strings with L.H.

P. 19.   Bar 1. Lead basses with R.H.

Bar 3. L.H. marks the *diminuendo* and phrasing. Decrease size of gestures in R.H.

P. 20.   Bar 3. *Crescendo molto* with broad *legato* gestures in R.H.
L.H. implements dynamics.

Bar 5. Cut off wood-wind and brass with L.H. Subdivide 3rd and 4th beat for the *Allargando*.

P. 21.   Bar 1. *Subito fffpp crescendo* shown by strong 1st beat
with the L.H. indicating the contrasting dynamic.

Bar 3. L.H. leads the brass chords. *fff dim.*

Bar 4. Subdivide the 3rd and 4th beats to ensure precision in strings. L.H. cuts off the brass.

Bar 5. Very small but precise 1st beat, increase intensity of 2nd beat followed by strong 3rd beat. Decrease
to 1st beat of

Bar 6. L.H. sustains wood-wind. R.H. directs strings
pizzicatti.

Bar 7. Finishing gesture *ppp*.

SOME HINTS ON TUNING UP

1 The conductor as well as the oboe player should always have a tuning fork, New Philharmonic A.

2 The oboe player must be ready and 'warmed-up' when the time comes to give the A.

3 Only one section of the orchestra at a time to take the A and tune up, the remainder of the orchestra to be silent. Start with the violins, then violas, cellos and finally the basses. Next the wood-wind section and then the horns and brass.

4 It is a good plan to make the strings all tune the same string at the same time, starting with the A, then the D and G, then the C for violas and cellos, and finishing with the E of the violins.

5 I heard Mengelberg, when he paid his first visit to England, insist on every instrument getting the A correct before he allowed the strings to complete their tuning.

6 Take great care to ensure correct tuning between members of the wood-wind section; especially the flutes and oboe. If a piccolo is included in the score, be sure that this trouble-some instrument is tuned correctly and don't be led astray by the old, old excuse 'It'll be all right when it's warmed up'.

7 Finally insist that when the A is sounded the players really 'tune up' and don't just take an approximate A and then continue playing flourishes and heaven knows what!

Index